From Talking to Writing:

Strategies for Scaffolding Expository Expression

A Landmark School Teaching Guide

Terrill M. Jennings
Charles W. Haynes

Landmark School, Inc.

Prides Crossing, MA

Landmark School, Inc.

Published by Landmark School, Inc.
P.O. Box 227
Prides Crossing, MA 01965

Library of Congress Cataloging-in-Publication Data

Library of Congress Card Number: 200109 2656
ISBN 0-9624119-8-1

Printed in the United States of America

Landmark School, Inc.

Contents

Landmark School, Inc.

Acknowledgments

We would like to thank our many friends and colleagues who helped make this book possible. We are grateful for the generosity of the Evander Lewis Foundation, Diane and Nicholas Lopardo, and Ruth Ellen Totten. In addition, we appreciate the mentorship we received from Professor Jeanne Chall at Harvard, who repeatedly encouraged us to "get these ideas into the hands of teachers as soon as possible."

Landmark School, Inc.

About the Authors

Terrill M. Jennings, Ed.M., is a founding teacher of Landmark Schools and has taught dyslexic students since 1970. Trained at the Harvard Graduate School of Education in its master's reading program, Ms. Jennings co-founded Landmark's expressive language program and is the head of the language arts department at Landmark's North Campus Middle School (ages eight through fourteen). Her particular focus is on developing techniques and strategies for teaching written expression.

Charles W. Haynes, Ed.D., taught at the Landmark School for fourteen years. He was a literacy tutor, a speech-language therapist, and coordinator of the Landmark School's Oral Expression Program. Dr. Haynes received his doctorate in reading, language, and learning disabilities at the Harvard Graduate School of Education. He is now an associate professor and a clinic supervisor in the Graduate Program in Communication Sciences and Disorders at the Massachusetts General Hospital Institute of Health Professions. The program, influenced by the same research and Landmark experiences that shaped this book, offers dual teacher certification in speech-language and reading based on a unified curriculum. Dr. Haynes serves on the board of directors of the International Dyslexia Association. His current research is in linguistic predictors of dyslexia and cross-cultural comparisons of learning disabilities.

Ms. Jennings and Dr. Haynes also co-authored *Thematic Instruction: A Teacher's Primer* (Landmark Foundation, 1992).

Landmark School, Inc.

About The Landmark School
Outreach Program

Established in 1977, the Landmark School Outreach Program provides professional development programs and publications that offer practical and effective strategies that help children learn. These strategies are based on Landmark's Six Teaching Principles and on over thirty years experience in the classroom. Members of the Landmark Faculty deliver graduate courses and seminars at the Landmark Outreach Center and on-site at school districts across the country. For more information about professional development opportunities and publications, visit our website at *http://www.landmarkschool.org* or contact the Landmark School Outreach Program at (978) 236–3216.

About the Landmark School

Founded in 1971, the Landmark School is recognized as an international leader in the field of language-based learning disabilities. The School is a co-educational boarding and day school with students, 7 to 20 years old, from across the United States and around the world. Within its highly structured living and learning environment, Landmark offers individualized instruction to elementary, middle and high school students. The School's program emphasizes the development of language and learning skills. Landmark students learn strategies for managing their learning differences so that they can realize their full potential both socially and academically.

Landmark Teaching Principles

Imagine . . . an instructional hour in which all students are interested and involved. The teacher motivates students by making the material meaningful to them. Information is presented in a variety of interesting ways that engage the range of learning styles in the class. The teacher builds opportunities for success by presenting information in small, sequential steps, and offers positive feedback as soon as students learn and apply a relevant new skill. The teacher provides examples and clear directions for homework, and sets aside a few minutes at the end of class for students to begin the homework assignment. During this time, the teacher answers questions and makes sure each student understands the task. In short, the teacher structures the hour so each student is challenged, works at an appropriate level, and leaves the class feeling successful and confident.

The Landmark School was founded in 1970 to provide this type of structured, success-oriented instruction to students with learning disabilities. For more than thirty years, Landmark teachers have continually enhanced and refined teaching strategies to help students learn more effectively. Landmark has shared its teaching strategies with public- and private-school teachers from all over the world through Landmark seminars. All students can and do learn from Landmark's structured, success-oriented instructional models.

At the heart of Landmark's instructional strategies and programs are six teaching principles. They are summarized below.

Teaching Principle #1:
Provide Opportunities for Success

Providing students with opportunities for success is key. Failure and poor self-esteem often result when teachers challenge students beyond their ability. Landmark begins teaching students at their current level of ability. This approach improves basic skills and enhances confidence. As Landmark teachers introduce each new skill, they provide basic examples and assignments to build confidence and keep students from becoming overwhelmed. As the information becomes more challenging, teachers assign students easier problems to supplement the more difficult ones. In this way, those students who are having trouble with the material complete at least part of the assignment while they work at understanding and learning

Landmark School, Inc.

to apply new information. Teachers provide students with whatever structure is necessary to help students be successful, such as study guides for tests, templates for writing, and guidelines for projects.

Only with a solid foundation of basic skills and confidence can students make progress. That is why it is key to provide them with opportunities for success.

Teaching Principle #2: Use Multisensory Approaches

Multisensory teaching is effective for all students. In general, it means presenting all information to students via three sensory modalities: visual, auditory, and tactile. Visual presentation techniques include graphic organizers for structuring writing and pictures for reinforcing instruction; auditory presentation techniques include conducting thorough discussions and reading aloud; tactile presentation techniques include manipulating blocks and creating paragraphs about objects students can hold in their hands. Overall, implementing a multisensory approach to teaching is not difficult; in fact, many teachers use such an approach. It is important, however, to be aware of the three sensory modes and to plan to integrate them every day.

Teaching Principle #3: Micro-Unit and Structure Tasks

Effective teaching involves breaking information down into its smallest units and providing clear guidelines for all assignments. This is especially important for students with learning disabilities. Micro-uniting and structuring are elements of directive teaching, which Landmark consistently uses with students. *Micro-uniting* means analyzing the parts of a task or assignment and teaching those parts one step at a time. Teachers organize information so that students can see and follow the steps clearly and sequentially. As students learn to micro-unit for themselves, they become less likely to give up on tasks that appear confusing or overwhelming. Consequently, these strategies enable students to proceed in a step-by-step, success-oriented way.

Teaching Principle #4: Ensure Automatization through Practice and Review

Automatization is the process of learning and assimilating a task or skill so completely that it can be consistently completed with little or no conscious attention. Repetition and review (spiraling) are critical. Sometimes students appear to understand a concept, only to forget it a day, week, or month later. It is not until students have automatized a skill that they can effectively remember and use it as a foundation for new tasks. Teachers must therefore provide ample opportunities for students to repeat and review learned material. For example, the Landmark writing process emphasizes practice and consistency. Students always brainstorm, map/outline, draft, and proofread in the same way. This provides them with an ongoing, consistent review of learned skills.

Teaching Principle #5: Provide Models

Providing models is simple, yet very important. It is one of the most effective teaching techniques. Models are concrete examples of what teachers expect. They do not mean that teachers are doing assignments for students. They are standards to which students can compare their own work. A model or example of a completed assignment serves as a springboard for students to begin the assignment. For example, teachers should give students a model of a sequential paragraph when teaching basic sequential paragraph writing.

Teaching Principle #6: Include Students in the Learning Process

Students are not passive receptacles to fill with information. They come to class with their own frames of reference. Their unique experiences and knowledge affect them as learners and should be taken into account. Therefore, during every exercise, teachers should accept student input as much as possible. They should justify assignments, accept suggestions, solicit ideas, and provide ample time for students to share ideas. Teachers should include students in assessing their own progress by reviewing test results, written reports, and educational plans. Creating and improvising opportunities to involve students in the learning process allows students to become aware of how they learn and why certain skills benefit them. As a result, students are motivated and more likely to apply those skills when working independently. In short, an included student becomes an invested student who is eager to learn.

CHAPTER 1

Foundational Theory and Methods

While some students learn to use language easily, a significant number do not. Despite teachers' best efforts to expose students to rich language experiences, authentic literature, and free writing assignments in the early grades, fifteen to twenty percent of students have extraordinary difficulty with oral or written language (Lyon 1997). These students experience frustration, lowered self-esteem, and reduced productivity. Their difficulties affect them, their teachers, and their parents (Paul 2000).

This book offers concrete strategies for teaching language that can help break the pattern of failure. It enables teachers to help students learn oral and written expressive language skills. It provides teachers with techniques and strategies for developing the expository language skills that students need to succeed. The book's systematic, explicit methods support students with language impairments while strengthening the language skills of every student in the classroom.

Our methodology emphasizes frameworks and scripts. *Frameworks* are linguistic templates with supports. Teachers find them helpful because they are based on *micro-uniting*, or small-step instruction. For example, frameworks for paragraph structures have embedded guides that help students form introductory and concluding sentences. Similarly, inset boxes that list transitional words help students combine sentences to make comparison-contrast statements. *Scripts* are samples of guided classroom discussion. They are embedded throughout the text to model the use of frameworks with expressive language techniques. Whenever possible, linguistic exercises are theme-centered and incorporate real-world vocabulary and concepts.

The strategies outlined in this book may indirectly enhance decoding and spelling; however, they are primarily geared toward developing language storage, retrieval, and formulation. Students who are in the earlier stages of learning to read and spell still need systematic training in speech-sound awareness and phonics (Adams 1990). Below-average readers additionally require multisensory instruction that is direct, intensive, systematic, and individualized.

At the time of this writing, there is a movement across the United States to hold schools accountable for students' development of language skills. As part of this commitment to raising standards, state school systems have adopted, or are in the process of adopting, criteria for measuring language skills. In states as geographically disparate as Texas, California, and Massa-

1

chusetts, comprehensive assessments require students to express their ideas in writing before they can progress to higher grades and graduate. These standards place greater pressure on teachers to ensure that all students perform at a proficient level. The strategies and techniques in this book are timely, then, as they will help teachers meet the new standards.

This book is intended as a resource for teachers with a range of background knowledge and teaching experience. Teachers with extensive knowledge of multisensory language instruction and expressive language methods can turn to the appendices, where we provide frameworks for scaffolding sentences, paragraphs, and essays. Teachers with less experience are advised to read the material below on basic expressive language techniques and related theory, then examine the scripts to see how they can use the frameworks in the classroom. The key is to pick and choose what best meets students' needs.

Cognitive Abilities That Support Language Expression

Verbal working memory, attention, and executive functions are important cognitive abilities that serve language expression. Understanding them enables teachers to evaluate their classroom methods more effectively. The paragraphs below define each function, outline the interrelationships, and link the functions to the instructional methods that follow.

Verbal Working Memory

Memory is the mind's system for taking in, modifying, storing, and retrieving information. When we temporarily hold information in consciousness and modify that information, we are using working memory. If the information is in the form of speech, then we are using *verbal working memory*. For example, when someone tells us a telephone number to write down, we use verbal working memory. We verbally rehearse the numbers to hold them in mind so we can get them down on paper. Also, when we read syntactically complicated sentences, we often convert them to internal speech. We hold chunks of those sentences in working memory and try to understand the meaning.

We also employ verbal working memory when we assemble phrases, clauses, sentences, and multisentence texts while speaking or writing. A student who is asked to formulate an if sentence about Lewis and Clark, for example, relies heavily on verbal working memory. The student formulates a string of words—a clause—and keeps the string of words in mind while formulating the rest of the sentence. If the student is successful, a meaningful sentence results: "If Lewis and Clark received support from the president, they would explore the Oregon Trail."

In general, students with a strong ability to hold and modify verbal material in memory are better able to formulate sentences and paragraphs. Students with weak verbal working memory often have trouble formulating spoken and written language. When teachers' writing instruction provides explicit support for verbal working memory, students with working memory difficulties are more likely to succeed.

Attention

Verbal working memory relies heavily on *attention*. To formulate a sentence, students must be able to focus selectively on words and switch their focus to different parts of the sentence in the presence of various auditory and visual distractions. For this reason, students who struggle with attention to verbal information usually have difficulty understanding or producing sentences and paragraphs. Teaching methods that focus and direct attention enable students to succeed with language.

Executive Functioning

To complete a procedure successfully—whether making a peanut butter sandwich, leaving a telephone message, or producing a sentence or paragraph–we need a plan. We also need to be able to check or monitor our actions to make sure we fulfill our plan. Planning and self-monitoring are *executive functions* that help us every day.

To produce the *if* sentence discussed above, the student needs a generic plan for how to order words in an *if* clause. In addition, the student needs to self-monitor to make sure that the sentence is accurate according to plan. Students with robust executive functioning skills tend to be better at making sentences and paragraphs. Students with poor language planning and self-monitoring are usually weaker at language formulation. For these reasons, the most effective teaching methods for sentence- and paragraph-level language production are those that aid key elements of executive functioning.

Interrelationships

Verbal working memory, attention, and executive functioning work in close relationship to each other, as Diagram 1: Functional Interrelationships shows. Each ability enhances the other, and a deficit in one ability often impairs the others.

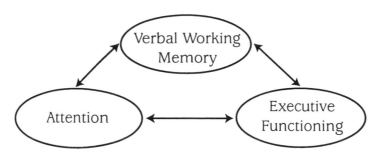

Diagram 1
Functional Interrelationships

In addition, these abilities overlap. For example, attention is critically involved in executive functions, particularly self-monitoring. Attention is also intimately involved in verbal working memory. Similarly, a student's knowledge of procedural strategies, which is an aspect of executive functioning, may influence his or her ability to handle information in working memory.

These interrelationships help explain why bright students diagnosed with attention deficit disorder (ADD) or attention deficit hyperactivity disorder (ADHD) often have difficulty checking their writing or holding verbal instructions in memory.

A Practical Analogy

The concepts of verbal working memory, attention, and executive functioning may seem abstract and not particularly applicable to teachers' daily work with students. A helpful analogy is to equate language formulation with a manual task, like assembling a grandfather clock. New parts for the clock come by mail (incoming stimuli). We retrieve others from shelves in our storage room (long-term memory). We assemble the parts on a workbench—our temporary workspace—using attention and working memory. At the same time, we use plans and monitor our accuracy (executive functioning). If we assemble the parts as planned, we produce a grandfather clock.

However, breakdowns can occur. If we do not selectively attend to clock parts at the right time, we may complete the clock case yet fail to insert the clock dial. If our storage room is disorganized, we may have trouble locating and retrieving the parts we need. If the workbench is too small, parts may fall on the floor while we work and become lost. If the surface of the bench is uneven, parts of the clock may slip and become glued in the wrong places. If our plan for building the clock is missing a page or we lack mastery of basic skills like gluing, drilling, and nailing, our result is imperfect. If we do not systematically check our plans, our clock might be incomplete or shoddily built. It follows, then, that strategies that strengthen our workbench, plans, storage, and attention to procedures give us a better chance to build our clock correctly.

Strengthening Techniques

As in the clock analogy, students' retrieval and formulation of language improves when teachers use aids to strengthen verbal working memory, attention, and executive functioning. Methods that enhance vocabulary development and retrieval include brainstorming, teaching the sound structure of words, aiding in the organization of background knowledge, cueing for word retrieval, and using thematic materials. These methods strengthen students' knowledge of word meanings and facilitate easy, accurate word retrieval and production. All are discussed in this book. Also discussed are sentence-, paragraph-, and essay-level techniques and strategies. These include:

- mnemonic strategies for recalling place concepts for where phrases and temporal concepts for when phrases

- systematic, hierarchical sequences for patterning sentences and paragraphs

- scripts for classroom language management procedures that ensure verbal rehearsal

- visual frameworks with category labels to cue production and self-monitoring of sentence and paragraph forms

- formulae for structuring production of topic and concluding sentences, as well as elaborating paragraphs

- inset boxes with words that cue formulation of sentences in a contrast paragraph, such as "but," "however," and "while"

- signal words for ordering a procedure, such as "first," "then," "next," "after that," and "finally"

In summary, most of the strategies and techniques we present are designed to improve students' development of formal expository language by aiding verbal working memory, attention, and executive functioning.

Techniques for Helping Students "Get the Words Out"

Imagine this scenario:

> A language arts teacher finishes reading aloud a story to her fifth-grade students. The teacher has illustrated a key scene in the story with a large, colored poster of a winged unicorn in flight.
>
> **Teacher**: Now write your own story about this picture. Be sure to use specific words to talk about what you see.
>
> **Jimmy**: Oh, what is that thing with the wings? . . . I know what it is . . . um, uh, hmmm . . . it's the imaginary horse with one horn . . . u-, ukinor, no, uni- . . . oh, I can't remember!

We all struggle for words at one time or another, particularly when we are fatigued or unfamiliar with the word we are trying to recall. For some people, however, difficulties with language create obstacles to expression. Difficulties can extend beyond isolated word-retrieval problems to the multisentence level, in terms of formulating sentences and discourse. Research and clinical experience suggest speech-language techniques that can aid students' language processing and formulation skills (Cohen, Sevcik, and Wolf 1999; Berninger 1999; Singer and Bashir 1999).

In the paragraphs below, we describe methods for enhancing vocabulary knowledge and word production that teachers can easily use. These techniques and strategies are:

- brainstorming
- teacher-provided cues and self-cueing
- organizing background knowledge
- developing student awareness of the sound structure of words

Brainstorming

Brainstorming is a classroom process for activating students' knowledge of concepts and vocabulary relating to a theme. Brainstorming employs overlapping and sequential phases: stimulation, guidance, and recording.

- In the stimulation phase, the objective is to activate students' prior knowledge and prime their "word pumps" for theme-related vocabulary. The teacher presents stimuli associated with the theme, such as photographs, prints, video clips, and objects. Students are encouraged to recall theme-related words from their own experience.

- In the guidance phase, the aim is to support students' efforts to recall words and concepts. The teacher accomplishes this by asking closed- and open-ended questions and by providing cues for word retrieval.

- In the recording phase, the teacher validates and elaborates on students' responses by writing them on the blackboard.

During brainstorming, the classroom atmosphere is often animated, with all three phases occurring simultaneously (Haynes and Jennings 1992). The words and concepts that students contribute, as well as the teacher's additions and elaboration, provide linguistic material for ensuing language exercises.

Teacher-Provided Cues and Self-Cueing Techniques

Some frequently employed *extrinsic (teacher-provided) cues* for word retrieval are gestural, pictorial, semantic, and phonemic or graphemic (Wiig and Semel 1984).

- Gestural cues, as the name suggests, involve use of pantomime to stimulate recall. For example, the teacher might imitate chopping movements to elicit the word "hatchet."

- Pictorial cues involve a visual representation or symbol that is usually static. For example, the teacher may use a picture of an eagle to elicit the word "eagle."

- For semantic cueing, the teacher provides meaning-related information about the target word. "Native American tribal gathering" might be a semantic cue for the word "pow-wow."

- Phonemic cues are sound structure hints, like the first sound or syllable of a word. If the student is struggling to retrieve the word "alligator," for example, the teacher might say "al-."

- The teacher might also give a graphemic cue, by saying the letter name *a* then the letter name *l*—or displaying these letters—to stimulate recall of the word "alligator."

Phonemic and graphemic cues tend to be easiest, because they hint at the target word's actual sound structure.

Self-cueing (intrinsic) strategies for word retrieval are used by the student rather than the teacher. Classic self-cueing strategies include visualization or imaging and recollection of time, place, and function. Visualization involves creating an internal, mental picture of the item the person is trying to name. For example, a student struggling to retrieve the word "saddle" can try to summon a mental picture of a brown, pommeled leather seat with stirrups hanging on either side. This mental image in turn may activate the sound structure of the word and enhance the student's retrieval (Bell 1991).

Another self-cueing strategy is to recall when an object is used. For example, cowhands use a saddle when they want to mount a horse. Another strategy is for the student to think about the place associated with the item. A saddle, for example, is associated with a horse or tack room. Still another method is to recall the function of the object. The function of a saddle is to provide stability and balance for a rider.

Visualization and recall of time, place, and function are useful methods for recalling objects' names. Teachers should directly and systematically instruct students with language difficulties to use these self-cueing strategies.

Techniques for Organizing Background Knowledge

Unlike Jimmy, who had difficulty retrieving the sound structure of the word "unicorn," some students have difficulty expressing themselves because they have incomplete or confused knowledge about the subject. For example, a student looking at a picture of climbers ascending Mount Everest might respond, "I think . . . um . . . they use those pick axes to hunt for animals." Similarly, the student might say, "The guy above . . . is, uh, using the string to pull up the ones below." In fact, the pointed tool is an ice axe, and climbers stick its point into the ice for stability. Also, the student uses "string" for "rope" and the general term "guys" instead of the more precise word "climbers." The student seems unaware that a rope is typically used to protect the lead climber from falling.

This student's response displays limited vocabulary and misleading background information about the topic. These problems are evident in the student's hesitancy, imprecise word choice, and misinformation. In such cases, teachers should focus on helping students correct, organize, and extend their vocabulary. In addition to providing direct, corrective verbal feedback, teachers can use graphic organizers as visual scaffolding for organizing and elaborating the student's vocabulary and concept knowledge. Examples of graphic organizers at the word and concept levels include semantic maps/webs, semantic feature charts, and organizational charts (Nagy 1988).

Teaching Awareness of the Sound Structure of Words

Another way that words are represented in the mind is by their *sound structure*—the melodic shape and the individual sounds and syllables that make up the words we hear and speak. Jimmy, the fifth-grader introduced at the beginning of this section, seems to understand the meaningful features associated with the picture of the unicorn. He said, "It's the imaginary horse with one horn." However, he struggles with retrieving the sequence of sounds in the word: "u-, ukinor, no, uni-."

One way to aid students' recall is to improve their awareness of the sound structure of key vocabulary words. If Jimmy's target vocabulary word is "unicorn," for example, the teacher can enhance his phonological awareness of that word by teaching him to recognize syllable number, stress, and order. The syllable-number technique follows:

> **Teacher:** How many syllables are in the word "unicorn"?
>
> **Jimmy**: Three.

A classic syllable stress task is modeled below.

> **Teacher**: Which syllable gets the main stress in "u-ni-corn"?
>
> **Jimmy**: The first syllable.

After Jimmy recognizes the number of syllables in the target vocabulary word, the teacher can build his awareness of the order of syllables in words by asking him to identify specified syllables. For example:

> **Teacher:** What is the third syllable in the word "unicorn"?
>
> **Jimmy**: Corn.

Simple techniques for helping students like Jimmy tune in to syllable stress include:

- engaging students in a motor response by having them tap out syllables

- increasing students' tactile and movement awareness of syllable pulses by placing their hands on the jaw and larynx (voice box)

- aiding syllable counting and sequencing by having students keep track of syllables on their fingers

All students, particularly those who struggle with syllable awareness, benefit from direct modeling, imitation, and practice of these techniques.

Production exercises, such as forward- and backward-chaining of syllables or phonemes, can also help students learn the sound structure of words. A script for forward-chaining the syllables in the word "unicorn" follows:

> **Teacher**: Say "u-."
>
> **Student**: U-.
>
> **Teacher**: Now say "uni-."
>
> **Student**: Uni-.
>
> **Teacher**: Say "unicorn."
>
> **Student**: Unicorn.

Backward-chaining runs in the reverse, building off the last syllable. Forward- and backward-chaining are simple, effective techniques for building students' familiarity and ease with articulating multisyllabic words. Again, direct modeling and imitation are often necessary for students to learn these methods. In turn, students' awareness of the sound structure of target vocabulary words can enhance their retrieval of those words.

Syllable-level methods are geared to a language arts classroom and work well with mildly impaired students. School-age students with more serious difficulties with sound structure awareness often require in-depth, individualized multisensory training at the phoneme and syllable levels (Lindamood 1998; Robertson and Salter 1995).

In addition to helping students produce words, teachers can develop students' spelling by implementing strategies that target sound structure. Students who are extremely weak, cryptic spellers are candidates for phonetic spelling. Phonetic spelling is an effective strategy for helping students write with spellings that, while sometimes inaccurate, are closer approximations to the target spelling. For example, a student who spells the word "rhinoceros" *r-s-r-n-a-k*, which is cryptic and indecipherable, might benefit from the four-step strategy below.

1. Identify the number of syllables in the word: Four

2. Write and number a blank for each syllable: __ __ __ __
                                               1 2 3 4

3. Spell the syllables phonetically and in order: <u>ri noss er us</u>
                                                    1 2 3 4

4. Combine the syllables into one spelling: <u>rinosserus</u>

While *r-i-n-o-s-s-e-r-u-s* is an inaccurate spelling, it is much closer to the target word than *r-s-r-n-a-k*. As a general rule, if students can spell the word using phonetic spelling rules or sight words they have already mastered, they should be required to apply the accurate spelling in sentence- and paragraph-level writing. If students cannot spell the word correctly using known patterns, the teacher may wish to credit them for phonetically correct spelling and then write the exact spelling directly above the phonetic version. For example:

Teacher's correction: rhinoceros

Student's original sentence: I saw a rinosserus at the zoo.

The strategies and techniques presented above effectively enhance students' word knowledge and retrieval. While the examples primarily focus on isolated words, the methods are useful for enhancing students' expression within a range of sentence- and discourse-level activities.

Teaching Language through Themes

When teachers anchor skills exercises in interesting and meaningful topics, such as life on the Serengeti Plains or the Civil War, students benefit from extensive review and practice of meaningful vocabulary and concepts. Consistent topics also allow students to focus their mental energy on learning the language patterns (Haynes and Jennings 1992). In the paragraphs below, we outline strategies for selecting, researching, and organizing thematic information. A *thematic unit* consists of topical source materials combined with linguistic exercises that elicit or contain key thematic vocabulary and concepts.

Selecting and Researching a Theme

A strong theme engages both the teacher and the students. A teacher who has a special interest in the topic is more likely to motivate students and create enthusiasm for learning. Similarly, if students are intrigued by a topic, they can better sustain their focus while learning skills. Themes are engaging when they:

- tap into students' background knowledge

- match the emotional maturity of students

- are introduced with materials that use language within students' semantic and syntactic grasp

- provide a variety of associated subtopics or strands (Haynes and Jennings 1992)

Once the teacher selects a theme, the next step is to research the topic. Research involves locating suitable materials and information as well as organizing the information by strands.

Locating Suitable Materials

For students with language problems, it is critical that thematic information be available in multiple modes: visual, auditory, and tactile-kinesthetic. In addition to the usual texts, students need to be exposed to information through pictures, interactive audio-visual aids, and hands-on experiences. Computer technologies, particularly interactive CDs and the World Wide Web, offer a range of multisensory sources of information. Teachers adapt this variety of stimuli to the individual student's interests and needs. With respect to content, themes that expose students to other cultures, such as the Wild West, Arctic Life, and Ancient Egypt, help students reflect on how the information fits into their own culture and environment.

Organizing Information by Strands

Students learn best when thematic information is pre-organized around subtopics, or *strands*. Sample schemes for organizing thematic information are illustrated in Diagram 2: Aspects of Human Culture and Diagram 3: Basic Human Activities. Both samples are based on the theme of the Wild West.

Diagram 2 shows how teachers might approach organizing Wild West thematic information about pioneers and Native Americans into strands. To implement this scheme, teachers ask students questions in each category. For example:

> **People:** What did pioneers or Native Americans look like?
>
> **Food:** What did people from each culture eat?
>
> **Buildings:** What did pioneers and different Native American tribes use for shelter?
>
> **Tools or equipment:** What kinds of tools did people from each society use, and for what purposes?
>
> **Clothing:** What kind(s) of clothing did pioneers or Native Americans wear?
>
> **Weapons:** What types of weapons did people from the different cultures use for hunting or protection?

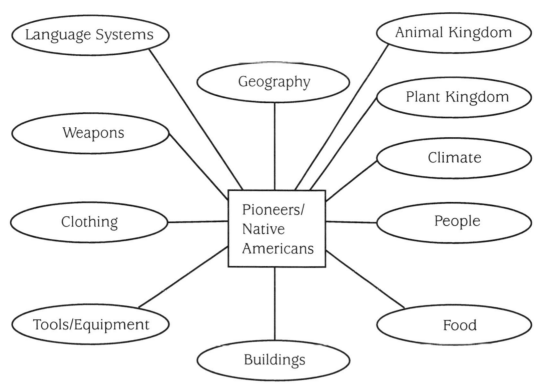

Diagram 2
Aspects of Human Culture

Language systems: How did pioneers or Native Americans communicate within or between their different cultures?

This scheme also helps teachers emphasize the natural environment in which a culture functions. Teachers can focus on basic aspects of the physical and biological environment that pioneers encountered as they ventured west or that surrounded the Native American cultures that pioneers encountered. For example:

Geography: What were the land and water forms surrounding the pioneers and Native Americans?

Animal kingdom: What animals did people from these cultures encounter?

Plant kingdom: What plants were particularly important to the pioneers or the Native Americans?

Climate: What was the weather generally like in the different places the pioneers and Native Americans lived and traveled?

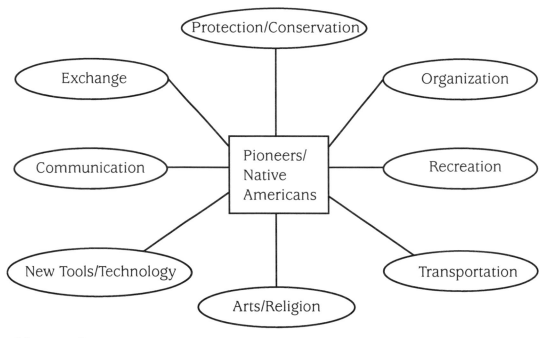

Diagram 3
Basic Human Activities

Diagram 3: Basic Human Activities depicts a more complex scheme for organizing thematic material. With this scheme, teachers can categorize information into social activities.

The broad questions below show how teachers can apply this scheme to the Wild West theme.

Protection/conservation: How did the pioneers or Native Americans protect themselves? How did they conserve their resources?

Organization: How were pioneer or Native American societies organized? What were the rule systems that governed pioneer or Native American behavior?

Recreation: What did pioneers or Native Americans do for recreation?

Transportation: What forms of transportation did the two cultures employ?

Arts/religion: What were the forms of pioneer or Native American art? What were their respective belief systems?

New tools or technology: What kinds of tools did each culture invent or employ?

Communication: What forms of oral or written communication did pioneers or Native Americans use?

Exchange: How did people in each culture purchase or exchange goods?

The two schemes described above provide teachers with systems for researching thematic material and, in turn, show students ways to categorize cultural information about the world. Teachers can integrate key vocabulary and concepts from the strands into oral and written linguistic exercises at the word, sentence, and paragraph levels. Theme-centered language teaching organizes semantic knowledge and reduces memory demands through semantic consistency. Perhaps most important, thematic materials promote students' interest by providing real-world vocabulary and concepts.

CHAPTER 2

Nouns, Verbs, and Prepositions

Overview

Many students, both with and without language difficulties, have only a rudimentary understanding of the type and function of words that make up sentences. Teachers need to help students understand the logical use of nouns, verbs, and prepositions in sentences, as well as the semantic relationships among them. In addition, students need to develop a range of vocabulary rather than repeat simple, familiar words. These skills pay dividends in more advanced expository writing, as variety in word choice and sentence structure adds to its effectiveness. Using themes to teach these skills not only provides new vocabulary, but expands students' range of words–the breadth and depth of vocabulary. Thematic units engage students in using meaningful words in meaningful contexts.

Nouns

To introduce rudimentary semantic concepts and basic syntactic elements, it is helpful to begin with concrete *nouns* because they are observable. They name objects, people, and places. They can be seen, touched, heard, smelled, or tasted. They have sizes, shapes, and parts. They can be drawn. They are associated with movement and can be categorized. They can be animate (alive) or inanimate (not alive).

As students experience and learn the meaning of new objects, they tend to focus on their distinctive features, such as shape and movement. Students eventually broaden their semantic knowledge and elaborate their depth of understanding about the objects. However, many students with language problems retain narrow, unelaborated meanings for nouns and lack an awareness that nouns have a range of adjectival characteristics. On a more subtle conceptual level, students need to know that nouns have synonyms and antonyms and can also be compared and contrasted.

Using thematic units to teach nouns enables students to learn a variety of topical words not encountered in their daily experiences. A script based on the Wild West theme follows.

> **Teacher**: Theresa, what is the category for the word "cabin"?
>
> **Theresa:** It's a building.
>
> **Teacher:** That's true. It's also a shelter, isn't it?

Teacher: Sam, is the cabin similar to a house?

Sam: Not really. They're both shelters, but a house is painted, is usually bigger, and has more windows. A cabin is built with logs and is much smaller.

Teacher: Bill, do you know the name of the other kind of building the pioneers built?

Bill: They built houses out of sod.

Teacher: You're right. The word you need has two syllables. Sod-.

Bill: I know. It's a soddy.

Teachers can use these techniques to aid students' retrieval and production of key theme-related nouns. Another effective method is the A-to-Z sheet.

The A-to-Z Sheet

Words are stored in memory by their sound structure as well as by their phonological, graphemic, and semantic features. An A-to-Z sheet exploits this knowledge to help students recall selected theme-related nouns that they and the teacher generate through brainstorming. The sheet is organized alphabetically and presents graphemic, phonemic, and semantic cues. Diagram 4: A-to-Z sheet uses the Wild West theme and the Lewis and Clark Expedition.

Diagram 4
A-to-Z Sheet

Graphemic Cue	Syllable Number Cue	Semantic Cue
b <u>buffalo</u>	3	Horned plains mammal, hunted by Native Americans and pioneers
C _ _ _ _ _ _ _ _	4	Large river between Oregon and Washington, on which Lewis and Clark traveled
J _ _ _ _ _ _ _ _ _	3	U.S. president who encouraged and advocated for Lewis and Clark's expedition
k _ _ _ _ _ _ _	2	Form of river transportation with a keel
S _ _ _ _ _ _ _ _ _	5	Native American who guided Lewis and Clark's expedition

Answers: Columbia, Jefferson, keelboat, Sacajawea

The A-to-Z sheet provides excellent practice of theme-related nouns. Teachers can insert nouns from any theme into its format. Teachers can also control the difficulty of the sheet by eliminating graphemic and syllable number cues and by assigning the sheet as independent rather than classroom work. While the focus of the A-to-Z sheet above is on nouns, teachers can easily apply the format to verbs, adjectives, and adverbs.

Verbs

At the basic level, students need to learn that a *verb* is an action word that describes the movement of a concrete noun. All concrete nouns have observable actions associated with them. Even nouns with static qualities can be defined by *non-movement*. For example, a door hangs, a mountain lies, and a tree stands. Students also need to understand that concrete nouns have functions or purposes. For example, ears listen, bark protects, and the sun heats.

Weak readers and writers need to broaden their range of action verbs rather than rely on such generic verbs as "come," "go," and "move." In addition, students need to use verbs precisely and correctly in given contexts. A useful way to broaden students' range of action verbs is to teach them in the context of an expanded sentence (noun plus action verb plus where or when phrase) and to use the inflected past-tense form of the verb. An expanded sentence forces students to make semantic relationships among elements. In the sentence "The horse galloped across the plains," for example, the action verb "galloped" is more precise than "went." It illustrates the noun's specific action in space.

Requiring an inflected form of action verb helps students:

- reduce initial confusion about noun-verb agreement in the present tense (e.g., the horses gallops vs. the horses gallop)

- reduce reliance on auxiliary plus verb plus *-ing* in the present progressive tense (e.g., the horse is/was galloping)

- learn regular and irregular past-tense verb patterns in sentence and paragraph contexts (e.g., gallop/galloped, stand/stood)

We have found it helpful to teach noun-plus-action-verb relationships in the following order:

1. animate noun plus action verb plus *-ed* (e.g., the horse galloped)

2. inanimate noun with no observable action plus action verb plus *-ed* plus optional prepositional phrase (e.g., the sky stretched over the plains)

3. inanimate noun with observable action plus action verb plus *-ed* (e.g., the branding iron branded the steer)

4. animate or inanimate noun plus function verb (e.g., a pair of alert ears listened for danger and the fire protected the cowboys from the wolves)

Inanimate-Noun-Plus-Verb Relationships

Students who are less flexible language users often cannot associate an action verb with an inanimate noun like "mountain" or "sky." Their typical response is that "it doesn't do anything" or "it doesn't move." Students need to learn a reliable strategy for making this association. One strategy is for students to learn the list of verbs below. These verbs are associated with inanimate nouns.

- leaned
- sat
- lay
- hovered
- hung
- stretched
- rested
- stood
- spread

Learning these verbs helps students make subtle associations, such as "clouds hovered," "leaves lay," and "mountains stood."

Prepositions

The standard definition of a *preposition* is a word used to show the relationship of a noun or pronoun to another word in the sentence. Prepositions and prepositional phrases pose problems for many students. A simpler way to explain a preposition is to call it a *position word*, one that tells the exact location of a noun. This introductory definition works because prepositions are usually associated with spatial (e.g., on the prairie) or temporal (e.g., at noon) relationships.

Prepositions require students to:

- recognize the precise location of objects that are fixed in a space (locative prepositions like "above" and "between")

- recognize movement or change of objects in space and time (directional prepositions like "into" and "toward")

- comprehend prepositions that indicate indefinite space (e.g., at school), indefinite time (e.g., about noon), and social pragmatic relationship (e.g., without the group)

- discriminate between similar-sounding prepositions, such as "in" and "on," "beside" and "behind," and "about" and "without" (Semel and Wiig 1984)

Diagram 5: Selected Prepositions by Level of Difficulty categorizes prepositions according to difficulty, as determined by Landmark School instructors working with language-disabled students. The list provides a sequence for teaching common spatial and temporal prepositions.

Students can practice the prepositions in Diagram 5 in phrases (e.g., on the plains) and expanded sentences (e.g., The herd of cattle grazed on the plains). Mastering a repertoire of prepositions and prepositional concepts provides students with a foundation for expressing spatial and temporal re-

Diagram 5
Selected Prepositions by Level of Difficulty

Level I	Level II	Level III
In	Below	About
At	Beneath	After
On	Across	Against
Up	Through	Along
To	Toward, towards	Among
Down	Underneath	Before
Around	Upon	Beyond
Near	Between	By
Under		During
Above		For
Over		From
Inside		Of
Outside		Until
Off		With
Into		

lationships in sentences and paragraphs. The exercises below, which provide modeling in the form of scripts, are formats for teaching prepositional concepts at each level of difficulty.

Describing the Precise Location of Objects

Teacher: (Places several common objects on the desk.) Let's see what you already know about prepositions, or position words. I am going to call on you one at a time and ask you if the pencil is in my hand or on my hand. I want you to answer in a complete sentence. (Places the pencil in her hand.) Bill, is the pencil in my hand or on my hand?

Bill: The pencil is in your hand.

Teacher: That's right. (Places the pencil on the desk.) Theresa, is the pencil in the desk or on the desk?

Theresa: The pencil is on the desk.

Teacher: Good for you. After the rest of the class takes a turn with "in" or "on," we'll review "up," "down," "over," and "above." Tomorrow, we'll review the prepositions we just worked on, and I'll add some new ones.

Follow-Up Activity

Teacher: We have been reviewing prepositions, or position words. What are some words that you remember? Let's start with you, Sam, and go around the circle. I'll write your prepositions on the blackboard and number them.

Class: In, on, up, down, under, near.

Teacher: I'm going to hand out sheets of blank paper. I want you to fold your sheet into six squares. Number the squares one through six, and copy the preposition that goes with each number from the blackboard. (Waits while the class completes the assignment.)

Teacher: Now I am going to read a series of sentences that tell where something is. You draw each sentence as best as you can. Be sure to pay close attention to the preposition or position word that you hear. The position word in the sentence also matches the word on your paper. Here is sentence number one: The clouds floated *in* the sky.

The teacher checks student papers for accurate use of prepositions.

CHAPTER 3

Adjectives

Overview

Children's development of *adjectives*, as with other elements of language, appears closely tied to their interaction with the world of objects and the quality of their interactions with primary care-givers. To understand fully what a specific object is, the child needs to focus attention on the object's features and attributes while examining it in a variety of ways and situations. Through experience, and perhaps with a mediating adult, the child recognizes that a ball has a color, size, and shape, and that it is a single object. Experiences like this, repeated over time, provide the child with a foundation for understanding and using adjectives in school.

However, children with language disabilities are not spontaneous language-learners. They often have problems analyzing and describing what they see and experience. As a result, they require explicit, highly structured teaching that centers on learning the adjectival features and attributes of nouns.

The classic teaching strategy for eliciting an adjective from a student might be:

> **Teacher:** Give me a word that describes a person, place, or thing. The word should answer the questions *how many*, *which one*, or *what kind of*.

Underlying this request are assumptions that the student:

- has adjectival information systematically stored in memory
- has strategies for recalling specific, accurate adjectives
- is aware of when and how to incorporate adjectives in oral and written expression

The Adjective Chart

To succeed in these operations, students with language disabilities need step-by-step instruction in the characteristics of adjectives. To aid this process, adjectives can be grouped into clusters and divided into twelve specific types. Diagram 6: Adjective Chart provides such an analytical scheme. With instruction, students can use the chart to recall and select a variety of specific adjectives to describe nouns.

Diagram 6
Adjective Chart

The Easy Four	*The Six Senses/Feelings*	*The Hard Three*
1. <u>C</u>olor	5a. <u>S</u>mell/5b. <u>F</u>lavor	10. <u>M</u>ade <u>o</u>f
2. <u>S</u>ize	6. <u>T</u>aste	11. <u>A</u>ge
3. <u>S</u>hape	7. <u>T</u>exture	12. <u>D</u>esign
4. <u>N</u>umber	8. <u>S</u>ounds like	
	9. <u>I</u>nner <u>f</u>eelings (emotions)	

The chart organizes adjectives according to approximate developmental level and the manner in which some cluster to describe specific nouns. Teachers introduce the chart to students in clusters, from the Easy Four to the Six Senses/Feelings to the Hard Three.

The first letters of the words are underlined; these provide mnemonic cues for specific adjective types. Teachers can offer these cues during the introductory learning phase. For example, students can recall the Hard Three Adjectives using the mnemonic *m-a-d*, because they are so tough that they can make students mad. As students gain proficiency in naming adjective types, teachers can remove the cues.

In initial phases of instruction, students may also benefit from blanks that cue specific adjective types. This technique teaches students to vary and stack adjectives. For example:

                      size   color

A subject like food can be described using the senses cluster: smell/flavor, taste, and texture. Mnemonic devices help students recall certain adjective types. Students can recall adjectives that describe smell/flavor, taste, texture, and sounds like, for example, using a sketch of the human face.

Frequent oral review and rehearsal enable students to recall the adjective types. By recording students' responses in a blackboard chart, teachers reinforce memorization.

The Easy Four Adjective Cluster

Prior to remediation, the descriptive vocabulary of language-disabled students may be limited to basic colors, a few words for size, and simple geometric labels for shape. Adjectives related to number tend to be limited to concrete words like "one" and "two." Intensive remediation around adjectives begins with the Easy Four Adjectives: color, size, shape, and number. Students review and practice these adjectives in phrases, expanded kernel sentences, and paragraph frameworks.

In the beginning, teachers need to ensure that students understand the concepts of color, size, shape, and number. Brainstorming is a diagnostic tool for teachers to discover what students already know about these adjective types, what they need to learn, and what misperceptions they hold. All students benefit from an oral discussion in a turn-taking format. When possible, teachers should ask students to provide synonyms for an adjective. This gives the teacher an opportunity to elicit subtle, specific descriptors. Using pictures and objects in the classroom helps students' memory as well as stimulates accurate associations.

Scripts for teaching synonyms and antonyms, requesting specificity, and eliciting general adjectival items for indefinite numbers follow.

Synonym Instruction

The teacher begins by writing these headings across the blackboard: color, size, shape, and number.

> **Teacher**: Let's see what you already know about color, size, shape, and number adjectives. I'll call on you one at a time and ask you to provide examples of each. OK, Sam, you're first. Give me a color adjective.
>
> **Sam**: Red.
>
> **Teacher**: Good. (Writes red in the outline on the board.) Do you have a synonym for the adjective "red," Sam? (Long pause.) I'm thinking of a word that has two syllables and begins with "crim-."
>
> **Sam**: I know. Crimson.

The teacher follows the same procedure with each student. When students' color adjectives are limited to basic words like "blue," "yellow," and "red," the teacher should encourage more precise synonyms.

Cueing for Specificity with Antonyms

The teacher holds up a stubby pencil and indicates the area from the eraser to the lead tip.

> **Teacher**: Bill, think of a size adjective that describes this pencil.
>
> **Bill**: It's small.

Teacher: That's true, but there's another word that is more specific than "small." It's the opposite of "long."

Bill: Short.

The teacher follows the same procedure with each student. The teacher requests specificity when students respond with overused words like "big" and "little."

Request for Clarification

Teacher: Theresa, think of a shape word that describes that door.

Theresa: Square.

Teacher: (Points to the window in the door.) What part of that door is square?

Theresa: Oh, that's right. The window is square. The door is rectangular.

The teacher follows the same procedure with each student. Note that further instruction is required for students to describe line shapes, such as "straight," "crooked," and "curly."

Associating the Easy Four Adjectives with Nouns

Once students understand the Easy Four Adjectives, teachers can show a theme-centered picture and ask each student to select a noun from the picture. As students offer nouns, the teacher writes them on the blackboard. The teacher next asks students to choose a noun from the blackboard and describe it with a color, size, shape, or number adjective.

The teacher writes the adjective before the noun and asks each student to read the adjective-plus-noun phrase. Teachers should require students to produce adjectives that are accurate and precise. Students cannot repeat other students' responses.

Less-able students may have difficulty shifting from one adjective type to another. In that case, teachers can request just one adjective type, such as color. As these students gain mastery, teachers can include other types of adjectives.

After the oral exercise, teachers can give students a worksheet that contains an Easy Four Adjective outline and a list of theme-centered nouns selected from the same picture. Here is an example:

The Easy Four Adjectives

1. Color

2. Size

3. Shape

4. Number

_____   clouds

_____   mountains

_____   chuck wagon

_____   horses

_____   cowboys

_____   river

Teachers ask students to think of a color, size, shape, or number adjective to describe each noun. Teachers can hang charts with examples of specific adjective types on the wall for easy reference.

If students cannot work independently, the exercise can be completed collaboratively. Students can fill it in with help from the teacher or by referring to an adjective chart on the wall. Using a reproduction of the worksheet on the blackboard or a transparency and overhead projector, the teacher invites each student to describe a noun orally, then writes the adjective on the blackboard before the appropriate noun. Students copy the adjective onto their worksheets beside the noun.

Once students expand one or more adjective types, they can stack them in pairs.

_____, _____   clouds

_____, _____   mountains

_____, _____   chuck wagon

_____, _____   horses

_____, _____   cowboys

_____, _____   river

When necessary, the teacher can cue students with adjective types. For example, the teacher might ask, "What is a color word for clouds?".

Elaborating on Color Adjectives

A fundamental principle in working with students with language disabilities is to make no assumptions. Teachers should first establish that students know the basic colors before introducing strategies for elaborating them. Then teachers can use the techniques below to broaden students' repertoire of color words.

The teacher creates different color families from a large assortment of crayons and hands a color family to each student. The teacher asks students to arrange the crayons on their desks from lightest to darkest. As a turn-taking activity, students name the colors. They can use the labels on the crayons. Examples are sea green, grass green, and so on. If the words are difficult to read, the teacher can help. Students then color in a series of objects, such as a row of houses or a string of balloons, using the different shades of color and label each object with its correct shade.

Once students are familiar with shades within a color family, they are ready to expand their color adjectives by associating a target color with a fruit (apple red) or vegetable (beet red). Linguistically sophisticated students may associate target colors with flowers (rose red), gemstones (ruby red), or other natural objects and phenomena (sunset red). These associations enhance and expand students' repertoire of color adjectives. The teacher can list the headings (fruit, vegetable, etc.) on the blackboard, as well as all the basic colors.

Teachers designate categories, such as fruits and vegetables, and colors. They list the categories as headings on the blackboard, as the example below shows, along with the basic colors in the left-hand column.

Target Color	Fruit	Vegetable	Flower	Gemstones/Objects/ Natural Phenomena
Red	_____	_____	_____	_____
Blue	_____	_____	_____	_____
Orange	_____	_____	_____	_____
Yellow	_____	_____	_____	_____

In a round-robin format, students fill in the table with words that fit the categories and are associated with the color.

> **Teacher**: I will give each of you a basic color word. Look at the categories on the blackboard and think of words that associate with the color. As you say the words, I will write them in the outline. Theresa, your color is "red."

Theresa: Apple is a red fruit. Tomato is a red vegetable. Tulip is a red flower. And I think I know a gemstone word . . . (Long pause.)

Teacher: It's a two-syllable word that begins with "ru-."

Theresa: Oh, I know. Ruby!

Teacher: Nice work, Theresa. Bill, can you choose one of the category words and combine it with the color word "red"?

Bill: Yeah, sure. Tomato red.

Teacher: Good, Bill. Now use "tomato red" in an expanded sentence about the Wild West. I have a picture of cowboys in a bunkhouse to help you.

Bill: The tomato-red blanket lay on the bunk one sunny morning.

Teacher: You are getting very good at this.

Some colors do not fit a category or the student may make an unrealistic color match (e.g., carrot blue and strawberry green). It is important for teachers to ask students to explain their choices and correct possible misperceptions. For example, many language-disabled students do not know a wide array of flower names. Teachers may need to teach them associations between common flower names and possible colors (e.g., white daisy, yellow dandelion, and blue iris). Teachers can hang colored illustrations from seed catalogues and seed packets on the wall for easy reference.

After the oral language activity, teachers can give students worksheets with the same headings and colors as on the blackboard. Teachers ask students to fill in the outline with nouns they identify by looking around the room, examining colored pictures of objects, or thinking of familiar words. They match their nouns to the colors on the worksheet.

Once students are comfortable with this task, teachers ask them to select nouns from colored pictures that center on a theme.

		Shade of Color	
Listed Noun	+	*Target Color*	*Familiar Noun/Thematic Noun*
Tomato		red	blanket
_____		_____	_____
_____		_____	_____

Next, students can write expanded kernel sentences that incorporate the descriptive phrases. Teachers can instruct students who have a firm grasp of the adjective word class to use a hyphen between the shade of color and its target color (e.g., ruby-red tulip).

Expanding Size Adjectives

Teachers need to make students aware that the concept of size includes four dimensions: weight, length-height, width, and depth. Brainstorming what students know about each of the four dimensions is a good initial activity because it surfaces difficulties with ambiguous concepts (e.g., the big snow/the deep snow and the long tree/the tall tree).

First-, second-, and third-graders need in-depth teaching to learn the dimensions. They need to be introduced to them one at a time with hands-on activities. Students in grades four to eight usually have a basic understanding of the dimensions, but their vocabulary may be limited to common words (e.g., big, small, and tall). Students with language disabilities often over-rely on concrete number words when referring to size and need encouragement to use more abstract vocabulary (e.g., the one-thousand-pound tree/the heavy tree and the ten-foot rug/the long rug). Teachers should ask for synonyms when appropriate.

As a turn-taking activity for first-, second-, and third-graders, the teacher can give each student an object and ask for an appropriate weight adjective.

> **Teacher**: I have given each of you an object. I want you to tell me what your object is and what it weighs. Please don't give me number words.
>
> **Sam**: This is a spoon, and it is light.
>
> **Teacher**: Good, Sam. (Writes "spoon" and "light" on the blackboard). Now describe the spoon using the size word "light."
>
> **Sam**: The light spoon.
>
> **Teacher**: Terrific! Can you say that in an expanded sentence?
>
> **Sam**: The light spoon rested in my hand.
>
> **Teacher**: Nice job, Sam. Now can you express that in a sentence about the Wild West?
>
> **Sam**: The light spoon rested in the cowboy's hand.

As a turn-taking activity for students in grades four to eight, the teacher can review the dimensions of size and ask students for specific adjectives that belong to each dimension type. First, the teacher writes these headings across the blackboard: target noun, weight, length-height, width, and depth. The teacher then records students' responses.

A script for this activity follows.

> **Teacher**: Each of you is going to choose a noun from the picture of a bunkhouse. Theresa, let's start with you.
>
> **Theresa**: OK. (Pause.) I'm choosing "porch."
>
> **Teacher**: Fine. (Writes "porch" under the heading "target noun.") Now look at the outline on the board and decide which of the dimension types can be used to describe a porch.
>
> **Theresa**: A porch is heavy.
>
> **Teacher**: That's right. (Writes "heavy" in the correct space.) Compared to what other object? Sam, do you have any ideas?
>
> **Sam**: Yes, I do. A porch is heavier than a door.
>
> **Teacher**: You're right. Theresa, how else can we talk about the size of the porch?
>
> **Theresa**: It's long and wide.
>
> **Teacher**: (Adds these words to the outline.) Good job. Bill, is the porch deep?
>
> **Bill**: Not really. We can't describe it that way.
>
> **Teacher**: Good for you. You could say a porch is high, but you don't usually think of it as deep unless you're a carpenter. You've just learned that not all objects can be easily described by all the dimensions. Theresa, choose two of the size words and describe "porch."
>
> **Theresa**: The heavy, long . . . the long, heavy porch.
>
> **Teacher**: I like the way you rehearsed the order of the adjectives. Your second phrase sounds better, too. Now put the phrase "the long heavy porch" into an expanded sentence. Use the picture to help you.
>
> **Theresa**: The long, heavy porch stretched across the front of the bunkhouse.

Once each student has a turn and the outline is complete, the teacher can instruct students to combine one or two of the size words with nouns from the blackboard outline or from a list of target nouns on an A-to-Z sheet (e.g., the strong, tall horse). The teacher can then ask the class to write expanded sentences that incorporate these phrases (e.g., The strong, tall horse galloped across the prairie one windy morning). The teacher should require synonyms when appropriate.

As this exercise shows, not all dimensions of size apply to all nouns. Deficits in spatial and temporal perception are commonly reflected in students' expression of size concepts (Wiig and Semel 1984). It is important to point out errors of perception or word choice (e.g., narrow horse/thin horse) and to illustrate correct responses with pictures and blackboard sketches.

Expanding Shape Adjectives (Grades One to Eight)

Rudimentary shape recognition takes place very early in a child's perceptual development. The child gradually perceives the geometric shapes of objects (e.g., round ball and square box). Over time, the child associates the features of geometric shapes with the nouns.

First-, second-, and third-graders need to learn the correct geometric shapes for a variety of objects (e.g., round button, square desk, and oval tomato). Sorting and matching tasks that incorporate oral and written language aid this learning. To introduce line-shape adjectives, the teacher can give each student short pieces of string, wire, or clay to model. The teacher demonstrates how to create different line shapes, and the students name the shapes with the aid of a word box on the blackboard. Students then create line shapes to illustrate words the teacher offers.

Students in grades four to eight may rely on simple shape words (e.g., round and square) beyond the time when their vocabulary should be more specific. By extending their awareness of line shapes, the teacher can enhance their vocabulary. As a turn-taking activity, the teacher draws four lines on the blackboard—jagged, straight, crooked, and winding—and asks students to identify them. The teacher then asks students for nouns associated with the adjectives. The teacher writes an outline on the blackboard and fills in the table as students respond. Here is an example:

Line Shape	Line Shape Name	Noun
∧∧∧∧∧	Jagged	_____
_____	Straight	_____
⟋	Slanted	_____
∿∿	Curved	_____

A script for this activity follows.

> **Teacher**: Bill, what word describes the first line shape?
>
> **Bill**: It looks like shark's teeth. (Realizes he must use only one word.) Sharp.

Teacher: Good try, but "sharp" describes how something feels. Let's look at what happens when a window is shattered by a base-ball. (Draws a broken window with a jagged edge.) The broken edge is j-. (Gives a phonemic cue.)

Bill: Jagged.

Teacher: Good. (Writes the word on the blackboard.) Now, what does "jagged" describe?

Bill: Glass that is broken . . . the jagged glass.

Teacher: That's correct. Sam, can anything else be jagged? (Shows a picture of a mountain range outlined in black marker.)

Sam: A mountain range . . . a jagged mountain range.

After the exercise, the class completes a writing exercise using the same format. Students identify the line shapes and provide their own nouns. The teacher can also ask them to write expanded sentences using the shape-adjective-plus-noun pattern phrases from the worksheet (e.g., The jagged glass rested in the window frame for several days). Pictures of settings that incorporate land and water forms are particularly helpful because they provide ideas for contours and object outlines. Teachers should ask students if a synonym can be substituted for a shape adjective. Teachers can help students in grades four to eight expand their vocabulary of shape adjectives by asking them to name an object for specific cloud, land form, and water form shapes (e.g., the cat-shaped pond and a dragon-shaped cloud).

Expanding Number Adjectives (Grades One to Eight)

When teachers initially ask language-disabled students for a number adjective, they usually respond with concrete number words like "one" and "thirteen." They have difficulty handling words that express indefinite quantity, such as "few," "most," and "several." These students are not aware that abstract number words fill the same role as concrete number words (Wiig and Semel 1984).

One simple strategy to teach abstract number words is for the teacher to ask students to guess how many paper clips are in a bag. The teacher should reassure the class that it is all right to guess because students will not be wrong if they do not say the exact number. In a turn-taking discussion, each student then takes a guess. A typical language-focused dialogue for this activity follows.

Teacher: Theresa, how many paper clips are in the bag? Please answer in a complete sentence.

Theresa: There are many paper clips in the bag.

Teacher: That's a good guess. Can you think of another word that suggests "many"?

Theresa: Yes. Several.

Teacher: Bill, how many paper clips are in the bag?

Another strategy for expanding indefinite number vocabulary is to teach students that nouns are associated by groups. Examples are a herd of cows and a pile of papers. Once students understand abstract number adjectives like "many" and "few," the teacher can introduce them to the group number adjective pattern. The teacher writes the outline below on the blackboard, which includes nouns that require a semantically accurate group number word.

a_____ of sneakers

a _____ eggs

a_____ of paper

a_____ of coins

a_____ of candies

a_____ of noise

A turn-taking activity that helps students think of appropriate vocabulary is modeled below.

Teacher: Sam, can you think of a number idea for "sneakers"?

Sam: A pair of sneakers.

Teacher: (Writes his response on the board.) Is there a synonym for "pair"?

Sam: A couple.

Teacher: How do we usually talk about two sneakers?

Sam: A pair of sneakers.

Teacher: Very good, Sam.

Teacher: Bill, how do we usually talk about a carton of eggs?

Bill: A dozen eggs.

Teacher: (Writes his response on the board.) What is different about this phrase, Bill?

Bill: It doesn't have the word "of."

After this activity, the teacher can distribute writing exercises with the outline from the board and a word box containing group number adjectives. Students match the adjectives with the target nouns. Another section of the worksheet instructs students to choose completed phrases and write expanded kernel sentences.

Additional exercises that address group number adjectives are those that fit categories, such as a group of animals or containers. Examples of animal groups are a herd of cattle and a school of fish. Examples of containers are a chest of gold and a barrel of oil.

Students with language disabilities have limited reading experience and so are not exposed to new adjectival words and expressions. Exercises that invite them to think about the relationships and recall what they know about group numbers to describe a variety of nouns give these students a valuable challenge.

The Six Senses/Feelings Adjective Cluster

After the Easy Four Adjectives, teachers can turn to sensory adjectives. Normally, we think of the five senses as smell, taste, touch, hearing, and sight. However, students with perceptual deficits may have problems interpreting the concepts expressed by the five senses (Wiig and Semel 1984). Therefore, teachers can modify the terminology to teach language-disabled students. The category, which is listed in Diagram 6, is called the Six Senses/Feelings.

- Smell and flavor are grouped because they are closely related and share vocabulary. Flavor is an important descriptor of food (e.g., chocolate and peppermint). Smell is generally associated with odor (e.g., smoky and fresh).

- The word "touch" is an abstract word that language-disabled students may confuse with the verb "to touch." This system uses the word "texture" instead.

- The word "hearing" can also confuse students. This system uses the more concrete phrase "sounds like."

- The traditional fifth sense, sight, is not among the Six Senses/Feelings Adjectives. To describe what something looks like, students rely on the Easy Four and Hard Three Adjectives, which express salient characteristics of a viewed object.

- A sixth "sense"—inner feelings—is a hidden sense that people recognize through body language and facial expression. Students with language disabilities often have great difficulty describing how they feel or how others feel. Their language is limited to simple, narrow words like "mad," "bad," and "sad."

To introduce the Six Senses/Feelings, teachers first need to ensure that students understand the concepts of smell, flavor, taste, texture, sounds like, and inner feelings. In turn-taking discussions, students brainstorm what they know about these adjective types by providing examples of each. Teachers can remind students that the smell/flavor adjectives are closely related and share vocabulary. Whenever possible, teachers should ask students to provide one or more synonyms for a word. Hands-on activities, such as food experiences, work well in teaching the Six Senses/Feelings vocabulary.

Expanding Smell/Flavor Adjectives

A helpful way to prepare students to expand their repertoire of smell/flavor adjectives is to brainstorm a variety of foods. Examples of food categories are fruits, vegetables, grains, baked goods and desserts, dairy products, meats, soft drinks, candy, and junk food. Core vocabulary sheets that target food nouns are helpful in organizing these word lists. Pictures to aid memory and word retrieval are also useful. Listing examples of specific foods, sorting a mixed list of food words into correct groupings, labeling groups of food, and adding food words to partial lists are a few activities that help acquaint students with the vocabulary.

Once students understand a variety of foods, they are ready to learn flavor words. The teacher writes this outline on the blackboard:

Color Adjective	*Ice Cream*	*Flavor Word*
Pink +	Ice cream =	_____
Green +	Ice cream =	_____
White +	Ice cream =	_____
Brown +	Ice cream =	_____

A script for this activity follows.

> **Teacher**: Sam, what flavor could pink ice cream be?
>
> **Sam**: Peppermint.
>
> **Teacher**: (Writes Sam's answer on the board.) Good. Now combine the color adjective "pink" with "peppermint ice cream."

Sam: Pink peppermint ice cream.

Teacher: Up to this point, you have been taught to place the color adjective directly before the noun. Why isn't the adjective "pink" next to the noun "ice cream" in this phrase?

Sam: Well, the ice cream is made with peppermint candy and that gives it its flavor.

Teacher: Nice thinking, Sam. If you say the "peppermint pink ice cream," you lose the meaning of the ice cream's flavor.

Teacher: Theresa, what flavor could white ice cream be?

Theresa: Vanilla.

Teacher: (Writes Theresa's answer on the board.) That's right, Theresa.

After this exercise, the teacher writes this outline on the blackboard:

Color Adjective	*Candy*	*Flavor Word*
Dark yellow +	Candy =	_____
Purple +	Candy =	_____
Red and white +	Candy =	_____
Black +	Candy =	_____

Here is a script for this activity:

Teacher: I know that all of you are familiar with candy, especially penny candy. The kinds of candy you think about when I say a color word will help you think of its flavor. OK, Bill, let's start with you. (Writes "dark yellow" on the blackboard.) What is the flavor of a candy that is dark yellow?

Bill: Lemon.

Teacher: Bill, the color I named is "dark yellow."

Bill: Ohhh, I know. It's butterscotch.

Teacher: (Writes Bill's answer in the outline.) Sam, what flavor is purple candy?

Sam: It's grape.

Teacher: (Writes Sam's answer in the outline.) Sam, what kind of candy comes in a grape flavor?

Sam: Ummm . . . lollipops and gumdrops.

Expanding Taste Adjectives

Students may have difficulty accurately associating taste words with foods because they lack familiarity with a variety of foods and do not consciously discriminate between a food's taste and flavor. Teachers can brainstorm with students to learn what they know about the basic tastes of food. Responses are usually limited to "sweet," "salty," and "sour."

Confusion between taste and flavor may also arise in discussion. It is helpful to tell students that taste is one of the original senses used to distinguish safe and satisfying foods from harmful ones, whereas flavor is a refinement of taste involving smell and is highly specific to the food it describes. Teachers should remember to ask for synonyms.

Teachers can teach students the basic taste adjective types in a turn-taking discussion. Students can recall the eight basic tastes with the mnemonic *b2-a-t-s4*, which stands for two *b* words (bitter, bland), one *a* word (acidic), one *t* word (tart), and four *s* words (sweet, sour, salty, spicy). The teacher writes this outline on the blackboard:

Basic Tastes	*(b2-a-t-s4)*
Bitter	*b*
Bland	*bl*
Acidic	*a*
Tart	*t*
Sweet	*sw*
Salty	*s*
Sour	*s*
Spicy	*sp*

This activity might run like this in the classroom:

Teacher: Theresa, can you name one of the eight basic tastes? Look at the letter cues to help you. Also think of the mnemonic *b-a-t-s*.

Theresa: Sweet.

Teacher: (Writes Theresa's response in the outline.) Is there a synonym for "sweet"? (Theresa looks puzzled.) Think of a three-syllable word that begins with s- . . . su-.

Theresa: Sugary?

Teacher: That's right, Theresa. Bill, name another basic taste.

Bill: Bitter.

Teacher: (Writes Bill's response in the outline.) Bill, what food tastes bitter? (Bill hesitates as he searches for a word.) Have you ever tasted unsweetened chocolate?

Bill: Not really. So unsweetened chocolate is a bitter food?

Teacher: Yes, it is. (Makes a note to bring in unsweetened chocolate bars used for baking.)

Once all eight basic taste adjectives are on the list, the teacher reviews them orally in unison with the class. The teacher then erases selected words, leaving only the first letter cues, and asks for volunteers to fill in the empty spaces. The teacher then erases all of the words and asks for volunteers to recite the eight basic taste adjectives in the correct order.

Next, the teacher distributes worksheets with the outline from the blackboard. To cue word retrieval, the teacher can include a word box with the basic taste adjectives. The teacher instructs students to describe a list of food nouns using two adjectives and to write their answers below the outline. In addition to a taste adjective, students may use color and flavor adjectives (e.g., an acidic, ruby-red tomato).

Expanding Texture Adjectives (Grades One to Eight)

An important attribute of a noun is its texture, which incorporates the sensations of direct touch and temperature. Students with language disabilities may have a weak repertoire of texture adjectives due to perceptual deficits or a lack of stimulating interactions with a wide variety of objects.

As a round-robin activity, teachers can ask students to brainstorm the concept of texture by examining objects in the classroom. Additional hands-on experiences may be necessary to enhance students' sense of touch as well as to make finer distinctions among sensations (e.g., the smooth pillow vs. the soft pillow). In addition, teachers need to have students consider the temperature of objects.

Once students in grades four to eight can easily provide texture adjectives for nouns in their immediate environment, they can apply their knowledge to what they see in pictures. First-, second-, and third-graders require direct experiences with objects for a longer period and will make the transfer to pictures more gradually. Remember to ask for synonyms when appropriate to build breadth of vocabulary.

Teacher: (Holds up a picture of a wagon train on the prairie and points to the withered grass.) Theresa, how would the grass feel if you touched it?

Theresa: Well, it's not green. (Long pause.)

Teacher: Would the grass burn if I lit it with a match?

Theresa: Yes. The grass is dry.

Teacher: Good. Now create an expanded sentence that uses the phrase "dry grass" as its subject.

Theresa: The dry grass burned under the hot sun all summer long.

Teacher: Thank you, Theresa. (Points to a wagon wheel.) Sam, how does the wagon wheel feel when you touch it? After you think of your adjective, create an expanded sentence.

Sam: Hard. The hard wagon wheel . . . (Pause.)

Teacher: (Gestures with a rolling motion.)

Sam: . . . rolled across the prairie for several hours.

Expanding Sounds-Like Adjectives

Students with language disabilities may have limited experience with the ways in which sound associates with objects. They need to become familiar with the distinct noises associated with animals and other common objects (e.g., a dog barks and a bell rings).

A strategy to teach sounds-like adjectives is to add the *-ing* suffix to an action verb (e.g., a barking dog). Having students place the adjective before the noun reduces confusion between the sounds-like adjective and the *-ing* form of the action verb, as in, "The dog is barking in the neighborhood." An initial turn-taking activity is for teachers to select different objects in the classroom and ask students to name the specific or motion-related sounds they make.

Some nouns do not make a sound when they are in motion or when they are still. Examples are clouds, sun, shadows, and dust. Students may need several lessons to make the most salient associations for sounds-like adjectives automatically.

Teacher: Sam, choose an object and tell us what sound it makes.

Sam: (Looks around the room.) Chalk. It doesn't make any noise, but if I use it on the blackboard, it taps.

Teacher: You're on the right track. Add an *-ing* suffix to "tap" and put "tapping" before the word "chalk."

Sam: Tapping chalk.

Teacher: Terrific! Now put the phrase into an expanded kernel sentence.

Sam: The tapping chalk distracted the students.

Expanding Inner-Feelings Adjectives (Grades One to Eight)

Adjectives that express emotions and feelings are often difficult for students with language impairment. They may have difficulty interpreting people's attitudes and emotions through facial expressions and nonverbal communications, such as gesture and touch. Direct experience with explicit instruction is a purposeful way to begin.

The most common inner feelings are happy, sad, shy, and scared. In turn-taking discussions, teachers can introduce first-, second-, and third-graders to such inner-feelings adjectives by using facial expressions, tones of voice, and postures. Students can be models as well. Another option is to use pictures that clearly denote the facial expressions of people engaged in a variety of daily activities.

Once students are familiar with the basic vocabulary for feelings, teachers can distribute worksheets with cartoon faces that show the facial expressions reviewed. The worksheet can also include a word box so students can select a word to match each expression.

Teachers can give students in grades four to eight an informal quiz to evaluate their understanding of the most common inner-feelings adjectives. Teachers first ask students to list four to six examples of inner feelings. Students then identify synonyms to expand their lists. Once students understand the most common emotions, they are ready to identify the inner feelings and attitudes of people and animals in theme-centered pictures.

Teacher: (Holds up a picture of a wagon train crossing the prairie on a late summer afternoon.) Bill, look at these pioneers. How do you think they feel?

Bill: Tired.

Teacher: Right. Do you have a synonym for "tired"? (Bill pauses.) I'm thinking of a word that has two syllables . . . w- . . . wea-.

Bill: Oh, weary.

Teacher: Good job, Bill. Sam, why are the pioneers so tired or weary?

Sam: They've been traveling in the hot sun all day.

Teacher: Good thinking, Sam. It's been a long, hot day for them. Sam, look at the wagon train leader. How do you think he feels with all the responsibility he has?

Sam: He's nervous.

Teacher: Right you are. Theresa, why is the wagon master nervous? Think about our discussions of life on the open prairie.

Theresa: Let's see. The wagon master is nervous because the pioneers have to find a place to camp before it gets dark.

Teacher: Yes, they all need to rest and there are problems if you travel in the dark.

The Hard Three Adjective Cluster

A third category of adjectives is the Hard Three: made of, age, and design. Students can recall the Hard Three using the mnemonic *m-a-d*, as they are hard to recall and can make students mad.

Some students have difficulty retrieving specific, accurate vocabulary from memory and, when asked to describe objects, rely on the easier adjective categories, such as color and size. These students seldom offer common object attributes—such as what the object is made of, age, and design—in their oral and written expressions. Before formally introducing these categories, teachers need to ensure that students understand the Hard Three category words. Some students may confuse the made-of category with parts of objects. Here is a typical example:

Teacher: (Holds up a pencil.) Theresa, what is this pencil made of?

Theresa: It has an eraser.

Teacher: That's a good try, but I'm not asking for the parts of things. Is this pencil made of glass?

Theresa: No, it's not. The pencil is made of wood.

Once students understand the category labels, they can share what they know about these adjective types by providing examples of each in a turn-taking discussion. Students may also recognize that they know many of the Hard Three Adjectives, but do not know when and how to incorporate them in their descriptions of objects. Hands-on activities, such as model-building and art projects, lend themselves to learning the Hard Three vocabulary. When appropriate, teachers should ask students for synonyms.

Expanding Made-of Adjectives (Grades Four to Eight)

A simple strategy to teach made-of adjectives is direct experience. Teachers can ask students to look around the room and choose an object. Students can also choose objects from high-quality pictures. Teachers ask students what each object is made of. It is important that students' responses be as precise and accurate as possible so teachers can clarify and correct any misperceptions. For example, a metal shelf offers a general description while a steel shelf offers a precise description.

Next, teachers can ask students to identify objects and what they are made of from theme-centered pictures. When the made-of adjective is part of a sequence that includes other adjective types, it should be positioned directly before the noun (e.g., an ancient oak tree and a red wool sweater).

> **Teacher**: (Holds up a picture of a pioneer prairie farm.) Sam, select an object from the picture and tell us what it's made of.
>
> **Sam**: I see a house.
>
> **Teacher**: OK. What was used to build it?
>
> **Sam**: It's not a log cabin. (Pause.) It's a sod house.
>
> **Teacher**: (Nods and writes Sam's response on the blackboard.) Sam, think of another adjective that describes "sod house" and use it in an expanded sentence. Use the picture to help you. (Holds up the picture again.)
>
> **Sam**: The dry, sod house stood on the prairie for many years.
>
> **Teacher**: That's terrific, Sam.

Expanding Age Adjectives (Grades Four to Eight)

The quality of age is inherent in nouns. When teachers initially ask students with language disabilities to provide an age adjective, they usually respond with concrete number words like "two" and "twelve." Occasionally they use colloquialisms; for instance, they might say "little kid" or "over the hill" when they mean "young" or "elderly." These students are not aware that abstract words like "young," "ancient," and "worn" can describe the age of people or objects.

First, teachers need to ensure that students understand the word "age." Then the class can explore the words "young" and "old" in a turn-taking activity. The teacher writes the headings "old" and "young" on the blackboard. A script for this activity follows.

Teacher: I want each of you to look around the room and choose an object. You can also choose people in the room. Tell me if your noun is young or old. Remember, I don't want concrete number phrases like "two years old." Bill, are you ready?

Bill: Yes. My word is "book." It is old. (Points to a well-worn dictionary.)

Teacher: How do you know that?

Bill: Well, it has an old cover and there are pencil marks on it.

Teacher: Good. You have looked hard at that dictionary. Do you know a synonym for "old"? (Pause.) It means very, very old.

Bill: Do you mean "ancient"?

Teacher: Yes, Bill. (Writes Bill's response on the blackboard.) Sam, Bill's dictionary is old. What is another synonym for "old" that means something has been used a lot? (Sam looks puzzled.) It's a one-syllable word that begins with the letter *w* and rhymes with "torn."

Sam: Worn.

Teacher: That's right. (Writes Sam's response on the blackboard.) The adjective "worn" describes objects or parts of things, like "the worn book" and "worn hands," but it isn't used to describe a person. We use "old" instead, like an "old farmer" or an "old grandmother." OK, Sam, what's another object in the room that is worn?

Sam: The chalk.

Teacher: Theresa, it's your turn. Choose something in the room that is young.

Theresa: Student. The young student.

Teacher: Good. What is a synonym for "young"?

Theresa: Teen-age.

Teacher: (Writes Theresa's response on the blackboard.) Right.

This exercise helps establish a core vocabulary for age adjectives. It also demonstrates how synonyms and antonyms can expand this vocabulary. Teachers can supplement theme-centered exercises that incorporate specific age adjectives in context with pictures. These language activities help students learn how and when to use age adjectives that are already in their vocabulary.

Expanding Design Adjectives (Grades Four to Eight)

Knowledge of design involves first-hand experience and thoughtful observation of objects. Designs can be very sophisticated. Most students with language disabilities do not have ready access to words that describe design. Although many objects are inscribed or printed with a design or pattern, these students do not appear to analyze them for this quality. They may confuse the idea of design with shape, *made-of*, or texture adjectives.

It is helpful for teachers to review a list of common design words (e.g., solid, plain, lined, striped, plaid, dotted, checkered, and floral). A simple strategy to teach basic designs is for students to brainstorm what they know about them. In a turn-taking activity, teachers ask students to identify the designs of objects in the classroom. Here is a script:

> **Teacher**: (Wearing a solid-colored sweater.) Theresa, does my sweater have a design or pattern woven into it?
>
> **Theresa**: No, it doesn't.
>
> **Teacher**: Do you know what we say when there is no design?
>
> **Theresa**: (Looks puzzled.) No, not really.
>
> **Teacher**: Does anyone have an idea? (No response.) Well, we say that the object is plain or solid. (Writes the words on the blackboard.) Please read the words "plain" and "solid" all together. (The class recites the words.) Sam, what is the design on Bill's shirt?
>
> **Sam**: It has a lot of lines on it running in opposite directions . . . and different colors. Is it striped?
>
> **Teacher**: Good try, but no. Bill's shirt is plaid. Sam, look at Theresa's skirt. (It is also plaid.) Is it the same design as Bill's shirt?
>
> **Sam**: Yes, her skirt is plaid.

Teacher: (Writes "plaid" on the blackboard and asks the class to repeat the word.) Terrific! Now you've got it! Bill, look at this sheet of paper. What is the design on it?

Bill: It has lines on it. It's lined.

Teacher: (Writes "lined" on the blackboard and asks the class to repeat the phrase "lined paper.") Bill, do we combine "striped" with "paper," as in "striped paper"?

Bill: That doesn't sound right.

Teacher: No, it doesn't work for the writing paper we use in school. That's called lined paper. When could we say "striped paper"? (No one responds.) We say "striped paper" to describe paper with stripes that we use to wrap gifts.

Once students know the common design adjectives, they are ready to expand their vocabulary. Teachers can ask students to analyze colored pictures and videos of animals or, if possible, live animals. Students describe their fur, skin, shell, scales, or feathers. The most common design adjectives for animals are "spotted," "mottled," "patchy," "blotched," "striped," and "barred."

To teach advanced design adjectives, teachers can have students examine fabric or a piece of clothing that repeats an image or geometric pattern. Teachers need to provide a variety of fabric swatches or clothing to give students first-hand experience with sophisticated designs. Good-quality magazine ads and clothing catalogues are also useful.

The teacher writes these headings on the blackboard: object, patterned, and noun.

Teacher: (Holds up a sports shirt with dogs printed all over it.) You all understand the most common design adjectives, like "striped," "plaid," and "spotted." Today I am going to introduce you to an overall design idea. Bill, what object do you see printed all over this shirt?

Bill: I see dogs. A dog shirt? (Pauses, shakes his head.) That doesn't sound right.

Teacher: Good, Bill. You're really thinking about the way words go together. The dogs form a pattern on the shirt. You could say the "dog-patterned shirt." (Writes this phrase in the outline.) Sam, what design is knitted in this sweater?

Sam: I see stars. No, snowflakes. I see snowflakes.

> **Teacher**: Correct. Now use the outline to describe the design of the sweater.
>
> **Sam**: The snowflake-patterned sweater.
>
> **Teacher**: (Fills in the outline.) Good.

After this activity, teachers distribute writing exercises for students to describe a variety of clothing using design, size, color, and *made-of* adjectives. On another section of the paper, teachers can ask students to use some of their phrases (e.g., long, plaid skirt) in expanded sentences (e.g., A long, plaid skirt hung in the closet for several weeks).

CHAPTER 4

Adverbs

Overview

A commonly accepted teacher's definition of an *adverb* is "a word that describes a verb by responding to the questions *how*, *when*, and *where*." However, this definition is too vague for many students to grasp. Many students' knowledge of adverbs appears closely tied to their knowledge of adjectives, as well as their understanding of temporal and spatial relationships—prepositional concepts. Before learning about adverbs, students need to learn to shift *where* and *when* prepositional phrases to the beginning of expanded sentences. In addition, students should be familiar with compound sentences and sentences that require a *because* clause.

When teachers expect students to understand, identify, and produce adverbs, they are assuming that students can:

- systematically store information about adverbs in memory

- use strategies for recalling specific, accurate adverbs

- incorporate adverbs in oral and written expression

Once students know that adjectives add information to the noun, they have a foundation for learning that adverbs add information to the verb. While adverbs usually end in *-ly*, it is important for students to know that not all words that end in *-ly* are adverbs (e.g., Sally and hilly) and not all adverbs end in *-ly* (e.g., always and often).

The Adjective-Adverb Connection

Teachers can exploit students' knowledge of the adjective groups—the Easy Four, the Six Senses/Feelings, and the Hard Three—by having students convert selected adjective types to corresponding *-ly* adverbs. This applies to students in grades six to eight. For example:

Adjective	*Adverb*
Quick + ly	Quickly
Rough + ly	Roughly

Teachers may need to provide a step-by-step analysis of concrete adverb types. Diagram 7: Adverb Chart provides an analytical scheme for students to recall and select appropriate adverbs to describe action verbs.

Diagram 7
Adverb Chart

M-W-F	*F-O-L-F*
1. How <u>m</u>uch	4. <u>F</u>eels like
2. How <u>w</u>ell	5. How <u>o</u>ften
3. How <u>f</u>ast	6. How <u>l</u>oud
	7. Inner <u>f</u>eelings

Strategies for teaching students to recall certain adverb types rely on mnemonic devices. Diagram 7 organizes adverbs according to the mnemonic outline *m-w-f f-o-l-f*. The outline corresponds to this nonsense sentence: On Monday, Wednesday, and Friday, I play folf. The "*m-w-f*" part of the outline helps students recall these adverb types:

- how <u>m</u>uch (e.g., greatly and slightly)
- how <u>w</u>ell (e.g., excellently and fairly)
- how <u>f</u>ast (e.g., rapidly and slowly)

The "*f-o-l-f*" part of the outline helps students recall these adverb types:

- <u>f</u>eels like (e.g., roughly and smoothly)
- how <u>o</u>ften (e.g., daily and regularly)
- how <u>l</u>oud (e.g., loudly and quietly)
- inner <u>f</u>eelings (e.g., happily and nervously)

In Diagram 7, the initial letter of each adverb type is underlined. These letters act as phonemic/graphemic cues for students to fill out the adverb chart independently in the early stages of learning. Teachers can also start by limiting the outline to the "*f-o-l-f*" cluster.

With frequent oral review and rehearsal, students can verbally fill in the adverb chart as the teacher records their responses on the blackboard. As students gain proficiency naming adverb types, the teacher can remove the phonemic/graphemic cues.

The "*F-O-L-F*" Adverb Types

Students with language disabilities need intensive remediation to master awareness and use of adverbs. They need to learn new and unusual adverbs that they did not acquire due to their limitations in reading. Teachers should start by stating that adverbs describe or add information to the verb, and they usually end in *-ly*.

A successful teaching strategy is to focus on adverb types related to texture (feels like), what something sounds like (how loud), inner feelings, and how often something occurs. Students understand the concepts of texture, sounds like, and inner feelings from their study of adjectives. Their understanding of "how often" derives from their knowledge of *when* prepositional phrases in an expanded kernel sentence (e.g., "every day" is synonymous with "daily").

Once students are familiar with adverbs in these categories, teachers can introduce them to adverbs that tell how much, how well, and how fast—one at a time. It may be easier for some students to learn about adverbs that denote speed first, including the adverbs "quickly" and "rapidly."

Teachers need to address adverb recognition and use in the context of phrases, expanded sentences, and paragraph frameworks.

Expanding How-Often Adverbs (Grades Six to Eight)

Students should learn the *how-often* adverb type first. The prerequisite is mastery of prepositional phrases that tell time.

First, teachers explain the similarity between a unit-of-time prepositional phrase and a single-word adverb. Then, in a turn-taking activity, students orally compose expanded sentences that incorporate the unit of time as a *when* phrase. After each student provides a phrase, the teacher asks for an adverb to replace it. Using synonyms helps students avoid repetition and dependence on familiar words. Here is a language-focused script for this activity:

> **Teacher**: Theresa, compose an expanded sentence with a time phrase. Look at this picture to help you. (Holds up a picture of pioneers crossing the plains.)
>
> **Theresa**: The tired pioneers traveled across the prairie for hours on end.
>
> **Teacher**: Nice work. Does "hours on end" mean the time spent traveling will never end? (Theresa nods.) Think of an adverb that begins with the word "end."
>
> **Theresa**: Endly. That doesn't sound right.
>
> **Teacher**: You're on the right track. You need one more syllable . . . "-less."

Theresa: Oh, I know. Endlessly.

Teacher: Good job! Sam, compose an expanded sentence that has a time phrase. Use the same picture Theresa did.

Sam: The oxen pulled the wagons into the river right away.

Teacher: OK. What adverb means "right away"? (Long pause.) It has five syllables and begins with "im-me-."

Sam: Immediately.

Teacher: Good. Bill, do you know a synonym for "immediately"? (Pause.) It has three syllables and begins with "in-."

Bill: Instantly.

Once students can replace a time phrase with an adverb, the teacher can introduce another *how-often* adverb pattern. Nouns that denote time become adverbs by adding *-ly*. For example, the noun "hour" becomes the adverb "hourly." The teacher writes the outline below on the blackboard, reads the first example aloud, then lets students supply the target adverbs.

Every day = day + ly = daily

Every hour = hour + ly = _____

Every week = week + ly = _____

Every month = month + ly = _____

Every year = year + ly = _____

Every season = seasonal + ly = _____

As a follow-up writing activity, teachers might require students to compose expanded sentences that incorporate *how-often* adverbs in place of selected time phrases. Once students share their sentences and the teacher corrects them, students can select an adverb from a word box on the same worksheet and write it over a *when* prepositional phrase.

Expanding Feels-Like Adverbs (Grades Six to Eight)

The foundation for *feels-like* adverbs is the texture adjective type. Students know that adding *-ly* to an adjective creates an adverb. The teacher asks students to generate texture adjectives and then add *-ly* to create *feels-like* adverbs. The teacher writes the outline below on the blackboard, then lets students supply the target adverbs.

Texture Adjective	*Feels-Like Adverb*
Smooth + ly =	_____
Rough + ly =	_____
Sharp + ly =	_____
Soft + ly =	_____

A script for *feels-like* adverbs follows. Note how the teacher uses antonyms and requires students to use the adverb in a sentence.

> **Teacher**: Bill, think of a texture adjective. (Long pause.) What's the opposite of the adjective "smooth"?
>
> **Bill**: Rough.
>
> **Teacher**: (Writes Bill's response in the outline.) Good. Now add an -*ly* suffix to "rough."
>
> **Bill**: Roughly.
>
> **Teacher**: Can you add "roughly" to an expanded sentence with a *where* prepositional phrase? (Holds up a picture of a wagon train.)
>
> **Bill**: The wagon rolled roughly through the prairie grass.
>
> **Teacher**: Theresa, think of another texture adjective.
>
> **Theresa**: Bumpy. The adverb is "bumpily."
>
> **Teacher**: (Writes Theresa's response in the outline.) Terrific! Can you use "bumpily" in an expanded sentence?
>
> **Theresa**: The wagon wheels turned bumpily over the rocks.

As a follow-up writing activity, teachers can distribute a worksheet that follows both the oral exercise and the outline on the blackboard and instruct students to think of texture adjectives that can be converted into adverbs. After this part of the assignment, teachers can ask students to write expanded sentences that incorporate *feels-like* adverbs (e.g., The pioneers traveled bumpily over the prairie).

Expanding How-Loud Adverbs (Grades Six to Eight)

The foundation for *how-loud* adverbs is the *sounds-like* adjective type, which includes such adjectives as "quiet," "silent," "soft," "loud," and "noisy." Students with language disabilities depend on these familiar adjectives to describe what something sounds like until they learn to add -*ing* to an action verb to create specific *sounds-like* adjectives (e.g., barking and snapping).

The word "loud" in the phrase "how loud" is part of a mnemonic to stimulate recall of other *sounds-like* adjectives (loud + ly = loudly). Asking students to use synonyms and antonyms helps expand this list. The teacher writes this outline on the blackboard and has students supply the target adverb:

Sounds-Like Adjective	*How-Loud Adverb*
Quiet + ly =	Quietly
Noisy + ly =	_____
Soft + ly =	_____
Harsh + ly =	_____

Here is a script for this activity:

> **Teacher**: Theresa, think of a synonym for "quiet."
>
> **Theresa**: A synonym for "quiet" is "silent."
>
> **Teacher**: (Writes "silent" in the outline.) Good. Now add the *-ly* suffix to form an adverb.
>
> **Theresa**: Silently.
>
> **Teacher**: (Writes "silently" in the outline.) Sam, think of the opposite of "silent."
>
> **Sam**: Noisy.
>
> **Teacher**: (Writes "noisy" in the outline.) Add an *-ly* suffix to form an adverb.
>
> **Sam**: Noisily.
>
> **Teacher**: (Writes "noisily" in the outline.) Good.

After the exercise, the class may complete a writing worksheet that uses the same format as the one on the blackboard. This worksheet instructs students to recall *sounds-like* adjectives and then add *-ly* to form adverbs. On another section of the worksheet, teachers can ask students to sort *sounds-like*, *feels-like*, and *how-often* adverbs from a mixed list in a word box. A third section of the worksheet may provide space for students to write expanded sentences that incorporate one of these adverb types.

Expanding Inner-Feelings Adverbs (Grades Six to Eight)

The foundation for *inner-feelings* adverbs is the *inner-feelings* adjective type. Students know that adding *-ly* to an adjective creates an adverb. Teachers ask students to generate *inner-feelings* adjectives and then add *-ly* to create *inner-feelings* adverbs. The teacher puts this outline on the blackboard:

Inner-Feelings Adjective	Inner-Feelings Adverb
Happy + ly =	Happily
Excited + ly =	Excitedly
Anxious + ly =	_____
Nervous + ly =	_____

A script for this activity follows:

> **Teacher**: Sam, there are two examples of *inner-feelings* adjectives on the board. You are quite familiar with these words because the class has learned a long list of these adjectives. How do you form an *inner-feelings* adverb from an *inner-feelings* adjective?
>
> **Sam**: You add an *-ly* suffix to an *inner-feelings* adjective like "happy" and it becomes "happily."
>
> **Teacher**: That's a good explanation, Sam. Now think of an *inner-feelings* adjective and create an adverb by adding the *-ly* suffix.
>
> **Sam**: Nervous . . . nervously.
>
> **Teacher**: (Writes "nervously" in the outline.) Good.

A follow-up activity is to ask students to write a variety of sentence types that incorporate adverbs and center on a theme, such as the pioneers. Teachers provide frameworks for students to create the sentences. Sentences may include expanded sentences, compound sentences that require the conjunction "and" or "but," and complex sentences that incorporate a *because* clause. Teachers can also make pictures available to help students recall salient nouns and their associated actions .

Expanding How-Fast Adverbs (Grades Six to Eight)

Action verbs have the inherent quality of speed, which is easily observed. To develop a repertoire of *how-fast* adverbs, students need to rely on the adverb "fast." It is important to tell students that the word "fast" is both an adjective and an adverb. As an adverb, "fast" does not take an *-ly* suffix and is an exception to the rule. Students need to know that not all adverbs end in *-ly*, and words that end in *-ly* are not always adverbs.

The teacher writes this outline on the board:

Fast   *Slowly*

Quickly   Sluggishly

Rapidly   Gradually

Here is a script for this activity:

Teacher: You know that synonyms and antonyms help us expand our vocabulary from one word to several words. The word "fast" in the phrase "how fast" is an adverb as well as an adjective. It is an exception to the rule about adverbs in that it doesn't end in an *-ly* suffix. We don't say "fastly." However, the adverb "fast" can help us think of other *how-fast* adverbs. (Pauses to be sure everyone understands.) Bill, what is a synonym for the adverb "fast"? Remember that your word needs to end in *-ly*.

Bill: Umm . . . quick . . . quickly.

Teacher: (Writes the word in the outline.) Bill, I like the way you thought about your word. You realized that "quick" needed an *-ly* suffix to be an adverb. Theresa, think of a word that's the opposite of "quickly." The word can be a synonym for "slowly."

Theresa: Oh boy, that's a tough one. (Long pause.)

Teacher: Theresa, the word I'm thinking of has three syllables. Sl- . . . slug-.

Theresa: Sluggish . . . sluggishly.

Teacher: Sam, choose one of the adverbs on the blackboard and compose an expanded sentence. (Holds up a picture of pioneers digging sod.)

Sam: The dirty, tired pioneers . . . Can I put "slowly" in front of the verb?

Teacher: Yes, you can. (Writes what Sam has dictated on the board.). The adverb is going to hover near the verb, isn't it?

Sam: (Reads what he has said.) The dirty, tired pioneers slowly dug the sod in the prairie.

Teacher: (Writes the sentence on the blackboard.) Good job, Sam. You have figured out another place to fit the adverb. It likes to hover around the action verb, doesn't it?

A writing activity that complements this lesson is to provide students with a worksheet that requires them to supply appropriate *how-fast* adverbs for a series of expanded sentences that center on pioneer life in the prairie. On another section of this worksheet, teachers may direct students to compose expanded sentences that incorporate *how-fast* adverbs independently.

Expanding How-Much Adverbs (Grades Seven and Eight)

How-much adverbs are abstract and more difficult to learn than other adverb types. Mnemonics can help. One strategy is to teach students to recall vocabulary associated with the size adjective type — particularly the dimension of weight, which is concrete and directly experienced. For example, "The backpack weighed heavily on my back" stimulates recall of weight adjectives, which become adverbs with the addition of *-ly*. Another example is, "The sweater was expensively priced." This sentence addresses the concept of price, or the money value of things. Using synonyms and antonyms also helps students expand their vocabulary of *how-much* adverbs.

The teacher writes these sentences on the blackboard:

> The backpack weighed _____ on my back.
>
> The sweater was _____ priced.

Here is a script for this activity:

> **Teacher**: I want you to think of weight adjectives before you think of a *how-much* adverb. Don't give me concrete numbers like "one hundred pounds." (Pantomimes bent shoulders and back, while taking a few steps.) My backpack is filled with several books. I am bent over because of the weight. Sam, think about how much the backpack weighs. Read the first sentence and give me a *how-much* adverb.
>
> **Sam**: The backpack weighed . . . heavy . . . heavily on my back.
>
> **Teacher**: (Writes "heavily" in the first sentence on the blackboard.) Terrific! Sam, what is the opposite of "heavily"?
>
> **Sam**: Lightly.
>
> **Teacher**: (Writes "lightly" in the first sentence on the blackboard). Bill, read the second sentence and give me a *how-much* adverb. Think about how the sweater was priced . . . what it cost.
>
> **Bill**: The sweater was priced at thirty dollars.

Teacher: Bill, I'm not asking for a concrete number. I want you to give me an adverb that tells how much. Is thirty dollars a lot of money? (Bill looks puzzled.) I'm thinking of an adverb that has four syllables. Ex- . . . expen-.

Bill: Expensively?

Teacher: Yes, Bill. The sweater was expensively priced. (Writes "expensively" on the blackboard.) Theresa, what is an antonym for "expensively"?

Theresa: Inexpensively.

Teacher: (Writes "inexpensively" on the blackboard). Sam, what is a synonym for "inexpensively"?

Sam: Cheaply.

As a follow-up lesson for this activity, teachers can prepare an A-to-Z sheet that introduces additional *how-much* adverbs, such as "excessively," "dearly," "exorbitantly," and "stingily." Teachers can ask students to select the correct adverb for a given sentence.

Expanding How-Well Adverbs (Grades Seven and Eight)

The last adverb type is the *how-well* adverb. One strategy is for teachers to ask students to think of the letter grades that teachers write on their papers and the adjectives that correspond to those grades. An *A*, for example, means excellent. By adding *-ly* to "excellent," students produce the adverb "excellently." Using synonyms and antonyms is also helpful to expand students' *how-well* adverb vocabulary.

The teacher writes this chart on the blackboard:

Letter Grades	Adjectives	Adverbs
A	_____	_____
B	_____	_____
C	_____	_____
D	_____	_____
F	_____	_____

The following activity is geared towards expanding *how-well* adverbs.

Teacher: I am going to teach you a strategy that will help you think of *how-well* adverbs. I'll call on you one at a time to think of adjectives that describe the letter grades on your papers. Think of the adjectives that teachers write on your papers to let you know how well you did on an assignment or test. After you give me the adjective, I'll ask you to add an *-ly* suffix to produce an adverb. I'll write your answers in the chart on the blackboard. Bill, what adjective describes an *A* letter grade?

Bill: Excellent.

Teacher: Good work, Bill. Now add an *-ly* suffix to create the adverb.

Bill: Excellently.

Teacher: Theresa, what adjective describes a *B* letter grade?

Theresa: Beautiful . . . beautifully.

Teacher: That's a good word. Do you know a synonym for "beautiful"? (Pause.) It's a three-syllable word that begins with "won-."

Theresa: Is it "wonderful"?

Teacher: Yes. (Writes "wonderful" on the blackboard.) What is the adverb form of "wonderful"?

Theresa: Wonderfully.

Teacher: Right. (Writes "wonderfully" on the blackboard.) Sam, what adjective describes a *C* letter grade?

Sam: Is it "average"?

Teacher: You're on the right track, but the word "average" is an adjective and cannot be an adverb. Think of a synonym for "average." The word begins with *f* and rhymes with "hair."

Sam: I know. Fair . . . fairly.

Teacher: (Writes Sam's response on the blackboard.) Bill, what adjective describes a *D* letter grade?

Bill: That would be "failing."

Teacher: You're making the correct association, but "failing" is one of those adjectives that can't be used as an adverb by adding an *-ly* suffix. Bill, if you get a *D* on your test, do you think you did excellent work? What's the opposite of "excellent"?

Bill: Oh, now I know. Poor . . . poorly.

> **Teacher**: Nice work. (Writes Bill's response on the blackboard.) Theresa, what adjective describes an *F* letter grade? How would you feel if you got an *F*?
>
> **Theresa**: I'd feel terrible . . . terribly!
>
> **Teacher**: That's right. (Writes Theresa's response on the blackboard.)

As a follow-up lesson for this activity, teachers can prepare a writing exercise that asks students to match an adverb to its letter grade. A second task is for students to sort an expanded list of *how-well* adverbs using "excellently," "fairly," and "terribly" as the target words. A final task might be for students to supply *how-well* adverbs in a series of sentences. For example, "The tired actor rehearsed his lines poorly."

Students who are learning *how-well* adverbs need to expand their vocabulary by searching for synonyms and antonyms in a dictionary or thesaurus. With teacher guidance, students can become sensitized to the precise meanings of *how-well* adverbs, especially in context.

Placing Adverbs in Sentences

At this point, students know that adverbs take their place directly after the action verb in a sentence. They know that the *how-often* adverb may replace the *when* prepositional phrase. They know how to shift *when* phrases to the beginning of a sentence and that *how-often* adverbs can work in that position as well.

During oral exercises, students may ask if an adverb can be placed directly before an action verb. The teacher writes these sentences on the blackboard:

> The anxious students sat quietly in their seats before the test.
>
> Several children ran quickly down the hall.

Here is a script for this activity:

> **Teacher**: Sam, read the first sentence on the blackboard. Place the adverb "quietly" in front of the action verb.
>
> **Sam**: The anxious students quietly sat in their seats before the test.
>
> **Teacher**: Bill, read the second sentence. Place the adverb "quickly" in front of the action verb.
>
> **Bill**: Several children quickly ran down the hall.

Once students can place adverbs directly before and after the action verb, teachers can demonstrate how most adverbs can be positioned at the beginning of a sentence. Here is a script for this activity:

> **Teacher**: Theresa, read the first sentence on the blackboard. Place the adverb "quietly" at the beginning of the sentence.
>
> **Theresa**: Quietly the anxious students sat in their seats before the test.
>
> **Teacher**: Do you like the way the sentence sounds with the adverb "quietly" at the beginning? You need to listen carefully to how the words are arranged in the sentence.
>
> **Theresa**: It's OK, but the sentence sounds better when "quietly" is near the verb. The anxious students sat quietly in their seats.
>
> **Teacher**: Sam, read the second sentence. Place the adverb "quickly" at the beginning of it. Think about how the sentence sounds to you.
>
> **Sam**: Quickly several children ran down the hall. I think the sentence is all right because you're not supposed to run in the halls. The adverb "quickly" attracts your attention.

A student might place an adverb at the beginning of a sentence when it is not the best choice in that context. An example is, "Heavily, the full backpack weighed on my back." The teacher should read the sentence aloud and ask the student to listen carefully to the way it is worded.

> **Teacher**: Sam, listen carefully to this sentence. See if you like the way it sounds. "Heavily, the full backpack weighed on my back." Does that sound right to you?
>
> **Sam**: No. I think it should say, "The full backpack weighed heavily on my back."
>
> **Teacher**: You're right, Sam. We have to listen carefully to the way words are ordered in a sentence just as we listen to the order of sounds in words when we spell them. In general, if you are in doubt, place the adverb after the verb.

CHAPTER 5

Sentences

Sentence Instruction: Rationale and Goals

The capacity to order words in phrases, clauses, and sentences is central to oral and written communication. The addition of one simple phrase can add critical information to a sentence. For example, "I will pick you up." sends a less complete message than "I will pick you up just before noon." Students who have not mastered the basic syntactic patterns of language are more likely to confuse or omit information when they listen, speak, read, and write.

When teaching *sentences*, it is important to:

- follow the general sequence in which children naturally acquire syntax, moving from simple to more complex patterns

- address both recognition and production

- address both oral and written language

Sequence

Teachers should introduce syntactic patterns gradually, moving from simple to more complex. Once students have a firm grasp of individual grammatical concepts (e.g., nouns and verbs), teachers can progress to kernel (noun-plus-verb) sentences (e.g., Dogs barked). Teachers can then introduce prepositional phrases, compound sentences, and complex sentences.

The patterns discussed in this section are illustrated with filled-in frameworks. The appendices provide blank frameworks, as well as detailed sequences for lessons on oral and written sentences.

Recognition and Production

Students who seldom include *time* or *space prepositional phrases* in their writing may have underlying difficulties recognizing these patterns. In addition, some students who can recognize or understand prepositional phrases may be unable to produce those phrases in their spoken language or writing. Speaking and listening skills underlie and interact with written language skills. For these reasons, it is important that students be able to recognize auditorily as well as speak the patterns they are required to read and write.

The Kernel Sentence

Articles

An *article* is a word that introduces a noun. The article "the" seldom poses a problem for students, and they usually use it to begin a sentence. Students also need to know that "the" may refer to singular and plural nouns. However, many students are unaware that the articles "a" and "an" are actually the same word and that they refer only to singular nouns. Before learning about a kernel sentence, these students need to learn that the article "a" precedes a word that begins with a consonant or consonant blend. The article "an" precedes a word that begins with a vowel sound–either a vowel or an unvoiced consonant, such as the *h* in "hour." A script for teaching "a" vs. "an" using the Wild West theme follows.

The teacher writes the articles "a," "an," and "the" on the blackboard and reviews their functions with the class. The teacher then holds up a picture of a bunkhouse from the thematic unit on cowboys in the Wild West and directs the class to look at it carefully. The teacher instructs students to think of nouns.

> **Teacher:** We are going to take turns naming what we see in the picture. I will write your nouns on the blackboard and you will tell me if the article "a" or "an" comes before it. Bill, what is your noun?
>
> **Bill:** Corral. (The teacher writes "corral" on the blackboard.) It should be "a" corral. (The teacher writes "a" before "corral.")
>
> **Teacher:** Good, Bill. Why should it be "a" corral?
>
> **Bill:** The word "corral" begins with a consonant.

The teacher hands out a sentence framework with a list of eight topic-related nouns from the thematic unit. The first task is for students to write "a" or "an" beside each noun. The second task is for students to select four of the noun phrases and write kernel sentences. A sample framework and a sequence for teaching the kernel sentence follow. Note that a "Word Box" provides cues for action verbs that associate with inanimate nouns.

KERNEL SENTENCE FRAMEWORK

Name: _____

Date: _____

Day: _____

> **WORD BOX for INANIMATE NOUNS**
> sat lay stood rested leaned
> hovered stretched hung spread

Article	Noun	Action Verb-ed
A	*cowboy*	*played his guitar.*

Construction of the Kernel Sentence

The teacher writes the *kernel sentence* framework across the blackboard: article plus noun plus action verb plus *-ed* (past tense).

> **Teacher:** We are going to compose kernel sentences using the framework on the blackboard. We'll use the bunkhouse picture to select our nouns. Let's start with Theresa.
>
> **Theresa:** Cowboy.
>
> **Teacher:** (Writes "cowboy" under "noun.") Good choice. What is your article going to be, "a" or "an"?
>
> **Theresa:** A.
>
> **Teacher**: (Writes "A" under "article.") Why did you say "a"?
>
> **Theresa:** "Cowboy" begins with a consonant.
>
> **Teacher**: Is "cowboy" alive or not alive?
>
> **Theresa:** "Cowboy" is an alive noun.
>
> **Teacher:** What is your action verb? What exactly did the cowboy do in this picture? Remember, we are using the past tense of the verb.
>
> **Theresa:** Played.
>
> **Teacher:** (Writes "played" as the verb in the sentence framework.) Yes, that's true, but we need to know what the cowboy played. Sometimes it's necessary to add a small noun to the verb so the meaning is clear. A cowboy played . . . ?
>
> **Theresa:** His guitar.
>
> **Teacher:** (Writes "his guitar" after the verb.) Nice work, Theresa. Now read the kernel sentence back.

As students compose kernel sentences, the teacher informs them that some verbs require elaboration in the form of a verb phrase with an object noun. At Landmark, this elaboration is part of the verb; we say "the verb is pulling a noun to it." Grammatical descriptions, such as "object of the verb" and "direct object," are too abstract for some students and may confuse them at this level of sentence construction.

As students provide each element of the kernel sentence, the teacher reviews the concept behind that element. With frequent practice and review, the rules that govern articles and elaboration of the action verb become automatic. It is important that the vocabulary students use in kernel sentences be as accurate and specific as possible to reflect the semantic relationships among the sentence elements. Once students are secure with their knowledge of the kernel sentence, the teacher can move on to expanded sentences that include prepositional phrases.

The Expanded Kernel Sentence

Sentences are the meaning-bearers of our language. When we link a topic-related noun and verb, we create a kernel sentence about an aspect of the world. Every specific noun has specific roles. If the theme is cowboys in the Wild West and the specific noun is "cowboys," students can create the following topic-related kernel sentence: "The cowboys herded the cattle."

When students are asked to expand on the kernel sentence to explain where and when the event occurs, they are required to elaborate on their understanding of the event — to express the specific role(s) of the noun in space and time. Given the above noun-plus-verb sentence about cowboys, students could express the following *expanded kernel sentence*: "The cowboys herded the cattle on the plains for months."

The expanded kernel sentence forces students to make semantic relationships among key elements within a sentence. It requires students to be accurate, precise, and complete in their understanding and expression of an idea.

Five Strategies

Five strategies help students learn the expanded kernel sentence. The first strategy is to focus on topic-related concrete nouns as the subject noun. Students with expressive language difficulties often depend on simple words, pronouns, and familiar proper nouns. In addition, their writing may rely on the first-person point of view (the "I" voice) to express what they know. Talking and writing about a topic-related noun as the subject of a sentence forces meaningful semantic relationships among sentence elements. Expressing ideas about a variety of topic-related nouns within a multiple-sentence exercise also provides a useful tool for expository writing.

The second strategy is to teach students to inflect a precise action verb. Students need encouragement to learn to inflect verbs rather than cling to the more familiar form, verb plus *-ing*. With respect to precise use, it is important that students accurately observe what they see and think of the most specific verb for the subject noun. Once students select a verb for a sentence in a multiple-sentence exercise, teachers can discourage them from repeating it to encourage variety.

The third strategy is to focus on Level I and II prepositions in spatial prepositional phrases (see Chapter 2, Diagram 5: Selected Prepositions by Level of Difficulty). The topic-related picture the teacher uses to stimulate prepositional phrases about space determines the prepositions students may use. Once students select a spatial prepositional phrase for a sentence in a multiple-sentence exercise, they may not repeat the preposition or the phrase. When appropriate, teachers should encourage use of synonyms.

The fourth strategy is to focus on prepositional phrases that express a time idea (*when phrases*). The concept of time is difficult for many students to express. They tend to repeat non-specific words and phrases (e.g., all the time, always, yesterday, today, tomorrow, morning, noon, and night). In addition, students frequently use clock time, such as "one o'clock," to express a time idea.

The teaching focus can be on the daytime clock, since most events related to a thematic unit occur during the day. Teachers can help students express time by dividing the topic into three phases: parts of the day, weather, and units of time. Once students use a temporal prepositional phrase in a sentence in a multiple-sentence exercise, they may not repeat it.

The fifth strategy is to provide vocabulary charts for each of the elements of the sentence for students' easy reference.

Keys to Success

- Use high-quality, theme-centered pictures to stimulate ideas and word retrieval.

- Brainstorm subject nouns and rehearse sentences orally before writing them.

- Use a turn-taking strategy to give all students an equal opportunity to respond and share information.

- Remind students that no noun, verb, adjective, or *where* or *when prepositional phrase* may be repeated in the same lesson.

- The student who composes the sentence reads it back orally and can make revisions.

- Remind students not to copy a sentence from the blackboard until the speaker is finished orally rehearsing it and making corrections.

• Make sure that students have enough time to respond.

The Spatial Prepositional Phrase

To get started on the spatial (*where*) prepositional phrase in an expanded kernel sentence, some students may benefit from brief exercises that focus on the structure of the prepositional phrase in isolation. For example, teachers might show a picture on the Wild West and ask students questions that focus on the exact location of objects.

Let's say the teacher is showing a picture of a bunkhouse with a corral behind it full of horses. On the fence rests a saddle blanket. On the porch of the bunkhouse are two cowboys, labeled "A" and "B." Cowboy A is sitting in a rocking chair, and cowboy B is leaning on the porch railing. A third cowboy, labeled "C," is sitting under a tree playing a guitar.

Question	*Where Prepositional Phrase*
Where is cowboy A?	In a rocking chair
Where are the horses?	In the corral
Where is cowboy C?	Under a tree

Students with a good understanding of the basic prepositions and the relationships among objects in space can learn the structure and use of *where* prepositional phrases in expanded kernel sentences. They do not require frequent, focused practice in isolated exercises.

Where Phrases (Grades Four to Six)

To start the lesson, the teacher writes an expanded kernel sentence framework across the blackboard: article plus noun plus action verb plus *-ed* plus *where* phrase. Note that the verb is in the past tense to teach inflection.

The teacher hands out the expanded kernel sentence framework. A sample of the framework and a script follow.

> **Teacher:** We have been working with prepositions, or *position* words, that tell the exact location of a noun. Now we are going to expand the kernel sentence by adding a *where* prepositional phrase. (Holds up a picture that depicts cowboys watching a herd of cattle on the plains.) Let's brainstorm a list of nouns before we compose the sentences. We'll go around the room until we have six nouns. As soon as I write each noun on the board, you copy it onto your paper. Be sure you write the word under the correct

Name: _____

Date: _____

Day: _____

EXPANDED KERNEL SENTENCE FRAMEWORK

WORD BOX for INANIMATE NOUNS
sat   lay   stood   rested   leaned
hovered   stretched   hung   spread

Article	Noun	Action Verb-ed	Where Phrase
The	cattle	chewed grass	on the prairie.

heading. I'll come around and check your work. Bill, let's begin with you, and then each of you will follow in turn.

Bill: Let's see. Cattle. (The teacher writes "cattle" under "noun." The class copies it.)

Sam: Sky. (The teacher writes "sky" under "noun." The class copies it.)

Theresa: Cowboys. (The teacher writes "cowboys" under "noun." The class copies it.)

Teacher: Nice work. Let's go around one more time.

The class brainstorms three more nouns and the teacher records them as above.

Teacher: It is important to listen as each of you orally rehearses your sentence. Be sure you wait until each sentence is complete before you fill in your framework. Bill, your noun is "cattle." Do you want to begin with "the," "a," or "an"?

Bill: I want to begin with "the cattle."

Teacher: Why did you select "the"?

Bill: There are many cattle in this picture. I have to say "the" to refer to them.

Teacher: (Writes "The" under "article.") Good thinking, Bill. What did the cattle do in this picture?

Bill: The cattle ate grass.

Teacher: Yes, that's true, but what is a more specific word than "ate"? Watch my jaw. (Makes a chewing gesture.)

Bill: Chewed grass.

Teacher: (Writes "chewed grass" under "verb.") Where did the cattle chew the grass?

Bill: On the prairie.

Teacher: (Writes the phrase in the framework.) That's right. Bill, read the sentence back. Then you may all copy it.

The class uses the same procedure to produce the rest of the expanded kernel sentences. Students use the nouns they select from the picture. The teacher guides sentence production with cueing strategies and guiding questions.

Where Phrases (Grades One to Four)

For students in grades one to four, it may be necessary to slow the pace of instruction to three or four sentences in one class period. In addition, students only provide one sentence element at a time in the turn-taking activity.

To start, the teacher writes the expanded kernel sentence framework across the blackboard: article plus noun plus action verb plus *-ed* plus *where* phrase. The teacher then hands out expanded kernel sentence frameworks. (The teacher may want to enlarge the framework format to accommodate the handwriting of younger students.) The class then brainstorms three nouns.

> **Teacher**: We're going to work with the three nouns on the blackboard that we brainstormed from the cowboy picture. No one is to write anything on their worksheet until I tell you to. Bill, which noun do you choose?
>
> **Bill**: I choose "cattle."
>
> **Teacher**: (Writes "cattle" under "noun." The class waits.) Now you write "cattle" under the correct heading, just as I have on the blackboard. I'll come around and check your papers. When we're finished, Bill will provide the article he wants: "a," "an," or "the." (Checks student papers.) Bill, which article do you want?
>
> **Bill**: The.
>
> **Teacher**: (Writes "The" under "article." The class waits for the teacher's direction before copying.) Good work. Sam, it's your turn. What is your verb? The cattle did *what*? (Holds up a picture of a cattle drive.)
>
> **Sam**: The cattle ate.
>
> **Teacher**: That's true, but what did the cattle eat?
>
> **Sam**: The cattle ate grass.
>
> **Teacher**: Yes, Sam, that's right. Can you think of another verb that's more specific than "ate"? Watch my jaw. (Makes a chewing gesture.)
>
> **Sam**: Chewed . . . chewed grass.
>
> **Teacher**: You did a good job watching me, Sam. (Writes "chewed grass" under "action verb plus *-ed.*" The class waits for the teacher's direction before copying.) If you need more space to

write the word "grass" on your worksheets, use the extra box under "chewed." Each sentence part has two spaces so you have room to write all the words. (Demonstrates using two boxes to write "chewed grass." Checks student papers.) Theresa, will you tell us where the cattle chewed grass?

Theresa: On the prairie.

Teacher: Good job, Theresa. (Writes "on the prairie" under "*where* phrase." The class waits. The teacher directs students to copy, reminding them they can use the second box to write "prairie.") When you've finished copying and I've checked your papers, Theresa will read the whole sentence. I'll help if she needs it.

The class follows this procedure to produce two more sentences.

Incorporating Adjectives

Once students demonstrate a clear understanding of the *where* prepositional phrase and the Easy Four Adjectives (color, size, shape, and number), they are ready to incorporate these adjectives into kernel and expanded kernel sentences.

The When Prepositional Phrase

Teachers can introduce prepositional phrases that express a time idea once students are secure in their knowledge of the spatial prepositional phrase and the Easy Four Adjectives. As students learn to expand kernel sentences with *when* phrases, teachers can gradually assign independent written work for them to practice and automatize what they know: nouns, verbs, adjectives, and *where* phrases. Diagram 8: Temporal (*When*) Prepositional Phrases by Level of Difficulty provides lists and a sequence for teaching three types of temporal phrases.

Parts-of-the-Day Phrases (Grades Four to Eight)

Teachers should conduct various isolated exercises that focus on practice and review of parts-of-the-day vocabulary before they ask students to incorporate these phrases in an expanded kernel sentence. One such exercise requires students to name the most common parts of the day according to the numbers on a clock face.

The teacher asks students to brainstorm parts of the day. The list may include both day and night vocabulary; however, the teacher explains that

Diagram 8
Temporal (When) Prepositional Phrases by Level of Difficulty

Level I *Parts of the Day*	Level II *Weather Time*	Level III *Units of Time*
At sun-up	On a sunny morning	A minute ago
During sunrise	One cloudy noon	An hour ago
At daybreak	During a rainy afternoon	Weeks ago
At dawn	After a windy sunrise	Day by day
In the morning	Foggy day after foggy day	Day after day
At midmorning	During the heat wave	Moments later
In the late morning	On a moonlit night	For centuries
At noon	Before the storm	For years and years
At noontime	One freezing dusk	For a while
At midday	After the rain shower	Once in a while
In the afternoon		A long time ago
In the early afternoon		Just now
In the mid-afternoon		Later on
On a late afternoon		Before long
At sundown		For a short while
At sunset		For a few minutes
At dusk		A moment earlier
At twilight		For days on end

prepositional phrases about parts of the day usually pertain to daytime events. The teacher then distributes Exercise 1: Parts of the Day.

The teacher asks students to match the words in the word box with the numbers on the clock face that have lines beside them. As a turn-taking activity, the teacher calls on students one at a time to match a word to a number, starting with sun-up. Once students match the numbers with the correct words, they complete the exercise on their own, copying the correct word from the word box beside each number. Students in grades one to

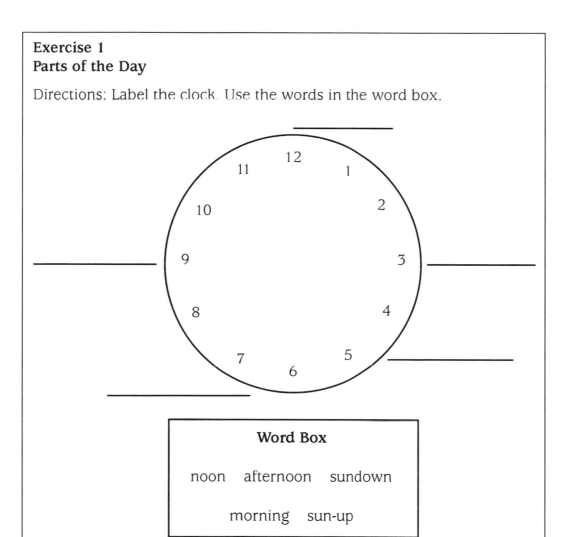

Exercise 1
Parts of the Day

Directions: Label the clock. Use the words in the word box.

Word Box

noon   afternoon   sundown

morning   sun-up

four may require close supervision and complete the task together, especially when copying the words from the word box.

Once students understand and can accurately name the most common parts of the day, the teacher can ask them to use the words in a phrase by completing sentences orally.

> **Teacher**: Theresa, your word is "morning." I want you to complete this sentence: I eat breakfast . . .
>
> **Theresa:** . . . in the morning.
>
> **Teacher:** (Writes the response on the blackboard). Good, Theresa. Now it's your turn, Sam. Your word is "noon." The bell for lunch rings . . .

Sam: . . . at noon.

Teacher: (Writes the response on the blackboard.) Good, Sam.

The next step is to expand students' vocabulary with synonyms for sun-up (e.g., sunrise, dawn, daybreak) and sundown (e.g., sunset, dusk, twilight), as well as the concepts "early," "mid-," and "late," which combine with the words "morning" and "afternoon."

When students can orally produce *when* prepositional phrases using parts-of-the-day vocabulary, the teacher distributes Exercise 2 for written practice. These follow-up exercises, when reviewed orally prior to independent writing, provide systematic practice and ensure automatic retrieval.

Expanding Theme-Centered Sentences with Parts-of-the-Day Phrases

The teacher prepares the blackboard with this outline:

Article	*Noun*	*Action Verb + -ed*	*When Phrase*
The	sun	rose	early in the morning.
_____	cowboys	_____	_____.
_____	corral	_____	_____.
_____	horses	_____	_____.

The teacher distributes the expanded kernel sentence framework, then shows the class a colored picture of a bunkhouse. Students analyze the picture for clues that tell what part of the day it might be. These clues could be the sun's position, shadows, or activities that logically occur during certain parts of the day. A sample framework and a script follow.

> **Teacher**: We have been learning how to produce *when* phrases that center on daily events. Now we are going to expand the kernel sentence by adding a *when* prepositional phrase that centers on our theme, cowboys in the Wild West. (Hands out expanded kernel sentence frameworks.) We'll follow the same procedure to produce these topic-centered expanded kernel sentences as we did for those that centered on daily events. We'll think of ideas about cowboys instead. Remember, once you've used a *when* prepositional phrase, you cannot repeat it. Bill, your noun is "cowboys."

> **Bill**: The cowboys watched the horses at sun-up.

> **Teacher**: (Writes the sentence on the blackboard.) I'm glad you added "the horses" to the verb "watched." Sometimes it's neces-

Exercise 2
Parts-of-the-Day Prepositional Phrases

1. Make a list of four parts-of-the-day words (e.g., sunset and noon).

2. Create *when* prepositional phrases by adding a preposition to a part-of-the-day word.

When Word (Preposition)	*Part of the Day*	*When Phrase*
At +	mid-afternoon =	At mid-afternoon
Before +	dawn =	_____
During +	an early sunset =	_____

3. Use *when* phrases from the list above to expand the kernel sentences below.

   The mailman delivered mail _____.

   The school bell rang _____.

4. Write expanded kernel sentences about the classroom.

Article	*Noun*	*Action Verb* + *-ed*	*When Phrase*
A	teacher	taught writing	_____.
The	children	_____	_____.

When teachers cover number adjectives, students learn that words like "many" and "some" can be used in place of an article. Teachers can then extend the exercise above by including a number adjective under the heading for articles, as follows.

Article	*Noun*	*Action Verb* + *-ed*	*When Phrase*
Many	desks	_____	_____.

Frequent practice and review of *when* prepositional phrases in the context of daily events gives students the skills to use these phrases in topic-centered material. Teachers can then require students to add one or two adjectives, depending on the pace and ability of the class.

Sentences

EXPANDED KERNEL SENTENCE FRAMEWORK

Name: _____
Date: _____
Day: _____

Easy 4	6 Senses	Hard 3
1._____	5._____	1._____
2._____	6._____	2._____
3._____	7._____	3._____
4._____	8._____	
	9._____	

WORD BOX for INANIMATE NOUNS
sat lay stood rested leaned
hovered stretched hung spread

WHEN PHRASES
parts of the day
weather
units of time

Article	Adjective	Adjective	Noun	Action Verb-ed	Where Phrase	When Phrase
The	vast	blue	sky	hovered	over the plains	that sunny day.

sary to add a noun to the verb to give more information. Sam, it's your turn. Your noun is "corral." Is "corral" an alive or not-alive noun?

Sam: It's not alive. The corral leaned after lunch.

Teacher: Good idea, Sam. Perhaps some of the horses pushed against it in the morning and loosened the posts.

The Weather-Time Prepositional Phrase (Grades Four to Eight)

Weather-time prepositional phrases (e.g., on a sunny day and one foggy morning) are another type of *when* phrase. Teaching strategies are similar to those for parts-of-the-day phrases and incorporate the rules for formulating expanded kernel sentences.

After students grasp *weather-time* phrases, teachers can help students use them independently with the exercises in Exercise 3.

The Units-of-Time Prepositional Phrase

A *unit of time* is an abstract concept that requires students to think about what they cannot readily see. Diagram 8 lists units-of-time prepositional phrases.

Teachers begin by asking students to name the common units of clock and calendar time, from smallest to largest (i.e., second, minute, hour, day, week, month, season, and year). The teacher writes the words in a list on the blackboard, then tells the class that these words are used in phrases. The teacher writes the following phrases on the blackboard as examples for the word "minute":

> for a minute
>
> a minute ago
>
> minute by minute
>
> minute after minute

Students then choose different words from the list and practice using them in phrases. The teacher writes the phrases on the blackboard as students orally formulate and rehearse them.

The teacher next provides students with sentences to complete orally using one of the phrases on the blackboard.

> **Teacher:** Theresa, please complete this sentence using the word "minute": The cowboy patted his horse . . .

> **Theresa:** The cowboy patted his horse for a minute.

Exercise 3
Weather-Time Prepositional Phrases

1. Make a list of five different kinds of weather (e.g., stormy and hazy).

2. Create weather-*time* phrases.

When Word (Preposition)	Weather Word	Part-of-the-Day Word	Weather-Time Phrase
On +	sunny +	afternoon =	on a sunny afternoon
After/before +	windy +	dawn =	_____
During +	cloudy +	sunset =	_____

3. Use *when* phrases from the list above to expand the kernel sentences below.

   The Pony Express delivered mail _____.

   The breakfast bell rang _____.

   A cow puncher chased a steer _____.

4. Write expanded kernel sentences using weather-*time* phrases.

Article	Adjective	Noun	Action Verb + -ed	When Phrase (Weather Time)
_____	_____	sun	_____	_____.
_____	_____	cowboys	_____	_____.
_____	_____	horses	_____	_____.
_____	_____	stream	_____	_____.

Teacher: That's right, Theresa. Bill, it's your turn. The horse galloped . . .

Bill: The horse galloped for an hour. I think that's too long . . . for almost an hour?

Teacher: Very good thinking, Bill. You have followed the pattern, but realize that galloping for an hour is very difficult for most horses. It is important to use the phrases that are listed on the board, but we can add words that help make what we want to say more accurate and logical. Let's compose expanded kernel sentences using these phrases on the board and see how we do.

The teacher writes the expanded kernel sentence outline below on the blackboard and then holds up a colored picture of cowboys herding cattle. Students follow the procedure for formulating expanded kernel sentences.

Article	*Noun*	*Action Verb* + -ed	*When Phrase*
The	cattle	grazed	day after day.
_____	dust	_____	_____.
_____	cowboys	_____	_____.

Exercise 4 provides follow-up exercises for teaching units-of-time phrases.

Exercise 4
Units-of-Time Prepositional Phrases

1. Make a list of different *unit-of-time* words (e.g., year).

2. Choose words from the word box to create *unit-of-time* phrases.

Units-of-Time Words		*Word Box*		*When Phrase*
years	+	ago	=	years ago

second minute hour day week month season year	for ago before by after

3. Use *when* phrases from the list above to expand these kernel sentences.

   The cattle grazed on the prairie_____.

   The rain fell_____.

   A cow puncher checked the water holes_____.

4. Write expanded kernel sentences using *weather-time* phrases.

Article	*Noun*	*Action Verb* + -ed	*When Phrase* (Weather Time)
_____	sun	_____	_____
_____	cowboys	_____	_____
_____	cattle	_____	_____

A Fully Expanded Kernel Sentence

Students who demonstrate a good working knowledge of the expanded kernel sentence are ready to produce a fully expanded kernel sentence. The teacher writes the expanded kernel sentence template across the blackboard: article plus adjective plus adjective plus noun plus action verb plus *-ed* plus *where* phrase plus *when* phrase. The teacher then hands out the expanded kernel sentence framework.

The teacher holds up a colored picture of cowboys herding cattle on the prairie. The teacher reviews the rehearsal procedure and reminds students to wait until each sentence is complete, including revisions, before copying it from the blackboard. Each student then brainstorms a noun, using the picture to stimulate ideas and aid in word retrieval.

Teacher: Sam, you brainstormed the noun "sky." What adjective types best describe the sky in this picture?

Sam: The large . . .

Teacher: Sam, think of a synonym that means "so large that there is no end to it."

Sam: (Looks at an adjective wall chart.) Vast. The vast, blue sky hovered . . . (Pauses.)

Teacher: Good so far, Sam. Look at the picture. What do we call this area beneath the sky?

Sam: The plains. Over the plains all day.

Teacher: Yes, that's true, but couldn't you provide more information by adding a weather idea?

Sam: OK, that sunny day. The vast, blue sky hovered over the plains that sunny day.

As the exercise proceeds, the teacher records students' sentences on the board, as follows:

Article	Adjective	Adjective	Noun	Action Verb + -ed	Where Phrase	When Phrase
The	vast	blue	sky	hovered	over the plains	that sunny day.
A	range of	ancient	mountains	stood	under the sun	day after day.

Throughout the exercise, the teacher encourages students to produce the most specific meaning for each sentence element. Oral rehearsal gives the teacher an opportunity to analyze student responses and heighten students' awareness of the possibilities when selecting ideas or words. Students experience a variety of perspectives and learn that there is more than one way to express ideas.

Teachers should assess whether each student is working to capacity rather than "plugging in" the sentence elements, as well as whether students are learning the logic of sentence elements. As students construct sentences, teachers should ask them to provide the category of a word, a synonym, or a word's corresponding adjective type (e.g., size and color). Such questions increase students' awareness of how language works.

Shifting Where and When Prepositional Phrases

The order of sentence elements can vary. Teaching students to shift the *where* or *when* prepositional phrase to the beginning of a sentence introduces them to the flexibility of sentence elements. To teach students how to shift a *where* or *when* prepositional phrase, teachers can follow the steps below.

1. Circle the *where* or *when* prepositional phrase in an expanded kernel sentence.

2. Draw an arrow from the circled phrase to the beginning of the sentence.

3. Strike out the capitalized first word of the sentence.

4. Capitalize the first word of the shifted phrase.

5. Move the period to its correct location.

6. Separate the shifted phrase from the rest of the sentence with a comma if it contains four words or more.

Compound and Complex Sentences

Once students master kernel sentence expansions and can shift *where* and *when* prepositional phrases within a fully expanded kernel sentence, they are ready to learn compound and complex sentence structures. It is helpful to introduce *compound sentences* in terms of the simple sentences that comprise them.

Compound Sentences with "And"

Teachers can get students started on compound sentence production by asking them to use the word "and" to link one sentence with another sentence that logically follows it.

they
The cowboys rounded up the cattle and ~~the cowboys~~ looked for strays.

calves
The cowboys rounded up the cattle and some ~~cattle~~ got lost.

The second sentence can add related information to the subject noun or the object noun of the first sentence. It can also take a pronoun (as in the first example above) or a synonym (as in the second example) to avoid repeating the noun in the second sentence. If students place a finger over the conjunction "and" in a compound sentence, they can see the two complete sentences on either side of it. Once students are familiar with this pattern, teachers can ask them to produce compound sentences independently with the aid of this template: noun plus action verb plus *-ed* **and** noun plus action verb plus *-ed*.

Students commonly omit the second subject noun when composing a sentence with this structure. Teachers need to distinguish a compound sentence with "and" from a simple sentence with a compound verb (e.g., The calf bellowed and ran).

Compound Sentences with "But"

The word "but" signals a contrast or an unexpected problem. While a compound sentence with "but" is similar to a compound sentence with "and," the meaningful relationship between the simple sentences differs.

The cowboys herded cattle, but the cattle stampeded.

When students place a finger over "but" in this compound sentence, they see two complete sentences on either side of it. They also see that "but" signals an unexpected problem: a cattle stampede. Once students understand this pattern, teachers can ask them to produce a compound sentence independently with the aid of this template: noun plus action verb plus *-ed* **but** noun plus action verb plus *-ed*.

Complex Sentences with "Because"

A complex sentence with the conjunction "because" incorporates a kernel sentence that tells about an event and a *because* clause that explains why the event happened. To form *because* sentences, students need to recognize that events happen for a reason.

> The cowboys herded the cattle because the cattle might run away.

Students need to recognize that the *because* clause is not a complete sentence; it cannot stand by itself. Once students know the *because* complex sentence pattern, teachers can ask them to produce a complex sentence independently using this template: noun plus action verb plus *-ed* **because** noun plus action verb plus *-ed*.

To help students distinguish among "and," "but," and "because," teachers can assign oral and written formulation tasks that begin with the same theme-related sentence start.

> The cowboys herded cattle and _____.
>
> The cowboys herded cattle, but _____.
>
> The cowboys herded cattle because _____.

Complex Sentences with When Adverbial Clauses

Many children, both with and without language problems, have difficulties processing, understanding, and producing sentences with temporal (*when*) clauses. A time idea in an adverbial temporal clause is more abstract than one in a prepositional phrase that expresses a part of the day or weather time.

Students who learned simple sentence structures systematically are better prepared to learn temporal adverbial clauses. They internalized the pattern of the main sentence and can use it as a reference point. In addition, they developed their ability to hold and manipulate longer sentences in verbal working memory through sentence expansion exercises.

Students need to master the *when* words that introduce the temporal or *when* clause. Teachers should introduce the ten key *when* clause signal words in the sequence below. It is roughly organized from least to most ambiguous.

> (1) as, (2) as soon as
>
> (3) when, (4) whenever, (5) while
>
> (6) until
>
> (7) once
>
> (8) after, (9) before
>
> (10) since

For the most part, a complex sentence with a *when* adverbial clause expresses a temporal relationship between two events. Students need to recognize that each of the ten *when* words signals the beginning of a *when* clause. They also need to know that a *when* clause is not a complete sentence. It expands a kernel sentence by providing *when* information. A *when* clause cannot stand alone.

The cowboys herded cattle near the water hole *as the clouds rolled by.*

The template for this sentence form is: noun plus action verb plus *-ed* plus *where* phrase plus *when* word plus noun plus action verb plus *-ed*. A sample of the expanded kernel sentence framework for the temporal clause follows.

The teacher writes the *when* words on the blackboard, then reminds the class that these words can be relied on to introduce a *when* or temporal adverbial clause. The teacher then writes the sentence outline below on the blackboard, including the subordinate conjunctions under the heading for *when* words.

Article	*Noun*	*Action Verb* + *-ed*	*When Word*	*Noun*	*Action Verb* + *-ed*
			as		
			as soon as		

The teacher asks students to brainstorm nouns from a colored picture that depicts a herd of cattle stampeding in a thunderstorm. The teacher does not write the nouns on the blackboard; the class recalls them by looking at the picture. Here is a script for the lesson:

Teacher: Sam, please create a sentence about this picture using the *when* word "as."

Sam: The cowboy patted his horse on the neck as he put on the saddle.

Teacher: (Writes the sentence on the board.) Yes, that's right, Sam. The cowboy can do those two things at the same time. Which is the main part of the sentence, Sam?

Sam: The cowboy patted his horse on the neck.

Teacher: Nice job. Is "as he put on the saddle" a complete sentence?

Sam: No, it's part of a sentence that tells when.

Teacher: What is the *when* word that introduces the *when* clause?

Sam: The word is "as."

EXPANDED KERNEL SENTENCE FRAMEWORK
Temporal Clause

Name: _____

Date: _____

Day: _____

WORD BOX for INANIMATE NOUNS
sat lay stood rested leaned
hovered stretched hung spread

WORD BOX for WHEN WORDS
as as soon as when whenever
while until once after before
since

Article	Noun	Action Verb-ed	Where Phrase	when word	noun	verb-ed
The	*cowboy*	*patted his horse*	*on the neck*	*as*	*he*	*put on the saddle.*

Sentences

The teacher repeats this procedure until each student understands the temporal adverbial clause. The teacher then implements the follow-up exercises outlined in Exercise 5.

Exercise 5
When Adverbial Clauses

1. Complete the following sentences.

   The cowboys herded the cattle on the prairie as _____.

   The horses chased the strays at the edge of the herd as
   soon as _____.

   Lightning struck the ground near the middle of the herd as
   _____.

2. Write sentences that include *when* adverbial clauses. Use the picture to choose subject nouns.

Article	Noun	Action Verb + -ed	Where Phrase	When Word		Noun	Action Verb + -ed
				as			
				as soon as			

3. Move the *when* adverbial clause from the end of the sentence to the beginning. For example:

   The horses chased the strays at the edge of the herd as soon as the rider gave the command.

   As soon as the rider gave the command, the horses chased the strays at the edge of the herd.

Complex Sentences with Object-Dependent Relative Clauses

Before formally introducing complex sentences with an object-dependent relative clause, teachers should cover the relative pronouns "who," "which," and "that." These pronouns replace nouns. "Who" replaces nouns that represent people. "Which" and "that" replace all nouns that represent the world of objects. In addition, students should be familiar with expanded kernel sentences, compound sentences, and complex sentences with a dependent clause.

The object-dependent relative clause describes the last noun in the verb phrase of the main sentence (e.g., The cowboy sang a song that calmed the herd). Students need to know whether a noun refers to a person or object and select the correct relative pronoun. Students' next decision is to determine what verb or verb phrase is associated with the object noun.

In oral exercises, the teacher reviews the relative pronouns using nouns from the thematic unit. The teacher lists the nouns on the blackboard, and students match each noun with one of the relative pronouns. The teacher reminds the class that these relative pronouns introduce an object-dependent relative clause.

Students next select nouns from a colored picture, such as one that depicts a stray cow and her calf in the brush with two cowboys watching in the background. The teacher writes this outline on the blackboard: article plus noun plus action verb plus *-ed* plus **who/which/that** plus action verb plus *-ed*. The teacher then distributes the expanded kernel sentence framework for the object-dependent clause. A sample follows.

Each student composes a sentence with guidance from the teacher. Here is a script:

> **Teacher:** Bill, please create a sentence using a relative pronoun. Remember that the relative pronoun needs to refer to the last noun in the main sentence.
>
> **Bill:** The cowboys found the cow and her calf, which was bellowing in the brush.
>
> **Teacher:** (Writes the sentence in the outline.) Good, Bill. In your sentence, what was bellowing?
>
> **Bill:** The calf.
>
> **Teacher**: What is the object-dependent clause in your sentence?
>
> **Bill:** Which was bellowing in the brush.
>
> **Teacher:** That's right. An object-dependent clause talks about the last noun in the main sentence.

The teacher repeats this procedure until each student understands an object-dependent clause. If necessary, the teacher can provide students with starter sentences (noun plus action verb plus object).

The teacher then runs the follow-up activities in Exercise 6.

EXPANDED KERNEL SENTENCE FRAMEWORK
Object Dependent Clause

Name: _____
Date: _____
Day: _____

Article	Noun	Action Verb-ed	who/ which/ that	verb-ed
The	cowboys	found the cow and her calf,	which	was bellowing in the brush.

Exercise 6
Object-Dependent Clauses

1. Circle the correct relative pronoun. Rewrite it as you complete the sentence.

   The cowboys herded the cattle on the prairie
   who/which/that _____.

   The cowboys chased the strays at the edge of the herd
   who/which/that _____.

   An angry cow charged the horse who/which/that

   _____.

2. Write sentences that include an object-dependent clause. Use the picture to choose subject nouns.

   | | | *Action* | *Object-Dependent Clause* | | |
   | *Article* | *Noun* | *Verb + -ed* | *Who/Which/That* | *Action Verb* | *+ -ed* |

3. Write a complex sentence using an object-dependent clause with the aid of this sentence outline:

   Noun + action verb + [who/which/that + action verb + *-ed*]

Complex Sentences with Subject-Dependent Relative Clauses

Of all the sentence structures we have reviewed, subject-dependent relative clauses are perhaps the most difficult for students to learn. For the first time, the subject noun is separate from its verb or predicate. For example: "The Blackfoot braves, who had gotten rifles from the French traders, used their weapons for hunting." This sentence form requires students to hold the subject (the Blackfoot braves) in memory, process a clause (who had gotten rifles from French traders), then link the main subject with its verb phrase (used their weapons).

The teacher's intonation is important for teaching this sentence pattern. Following standard procedures for oral rehearsal and guided follow-up activities is also important.

The teacher tells students they are going to use a subject-dependent relative clause to talk about a subject noun from the thematic unit. Students need to remember that once the subject noun is followed by a clause, the subject stills needs its verb. The teacher also reviews the relative pronouns that introduce a subject-dependent relative clause.

The teacher writes this sentence outline on the board:

Article	Noun	Who/Which/That + Action Verb + -ed	Action Verb + -ed
The	cowboy,	who entered the corral,	roped his horse.

The teacher covers the subject-dependent clause so students can see the kernel sentence (the main noun and its verb). The teacher then reveals the clause and uses vocal intonation to model how the clause talks about the subject noun. The teacher emphasizes "the cowboy," pauses, says "who entered the corral" (the subject-dependent clause) in a soft voice, pauses again, then says "roped his horse" (the main verb phrase or predicate) in a strong voice. These vocal dynamics help students hear how to direct this sentence pattern when they read and write it.

The teacher distributes the expanded kernel sentence framework for the subject-dependent clause. A sample follows on the next page.

Each student then composes a sentence with guidance from the teacher, as in the script below.

> **Teacher:** Theresa, please choose a noun from the picture and compose a sentence with a subject-dependent clause. Remember that the subject-dependent clause talks about the subject noun. Be sure to choose a noun you feel comfortable with. You have the background knowledge to support what you want to say.
>
> **Theresa:** Several cattle . . .
>
> **Teacher:** (Writes Theresa's words in the template on the blackboard. A long pause follows.) Theresa, you can talk about the cattle by providing an action verb or by describing them. Remember, the relative clause in a sentence talks about the noun by adding information to it.
>
> **Theresa:** . . . that were thirsty . . .
>
> **Teacher:** (Writes Theresa's words in the template. Another long pause.) That's good so far. You need to think about what the cattle did. You said they were thirsty, so what is a logical action for the cattle to take?
>
> **Theresa:** . . . wandered to a water hole.
>
> **Teacher:** (Writes Theresa's words in the template). Yes. Now I know which cattle in the herd you are talking about. Please read the sentence back and use the vocal dynamics I modeled for you.

EXPANDED KERNEL SENTENCE FRAMEWORK

Subject Dependent Clause

Name: _____

Date: _____

Day: _____

Article	Noun,	who/which/ that	verb-ed,	Action Verb-ed
The	*cowboy,*	*who*	*entered the corral,*	*roped his horse.*

The teacher continues this procedure until each student understands the subject-dependent relative clause, then distributes Exercise 7.

Exercise 7
Subject-Dependent Clauses

1. Circle the correct relative pronoun. Rewrite it as you complete the clause.

   The cowboys, who/which/that _____, herded the cattle.

   The cowboys, who/which/that _____, chased the strays.

   An angry cow, who/which/that _____, charged the horse.

2. Write sentences that use a subject-dependent relative clause. Use the picture to choose your subject nouns.

   Article   Noun   Who/Which/That + Action Verb + -ed   Action Verb + -ed

3. Write a complex sentence using a subject-dependent clause with the aid of the sentence template below.

   Noun + who/which/that + action verb + *-ed* + action verb + *-ed*

CHAPTER 6

Expository Paragraph Frameworks

Overview

During the first years of grade school, teachers typically focus most students' writing on the story to convey information. Much of what students read in texts is written in this narrative style (Caswell and Duke 1998). However, by the time students reach the fourth grade, most textbooks are written in expository form. Formal expository writing requires a variety of linguistic and expository structures. To generate expository writing, students need sophisticated language, the ability to make salient relationships, and content information. By middle school, students are expected to write proficiently—to plan and produce well-organized, coherent, knowledge-based texts.

Our experience in working with students with language and learning disabilities is that they are motivated to write expository texts because they can state factual information in a straightforward manner. Thematic units provide a rich context that captures students' interest and enables them to make connections between their background knowledge and content. Students are eager to share the facts they learn in a thematic unit. They are invested in writing about what they know.

To become proficient readers and writers of expository text, students need high levels of text awareness and mastery of paragraph-writing strategies. They need to internalize a variety of paragraph frameworks to prompt production so they can devote more attention to paragraph content as they write.

This chapter provides detailed instruction and rich contextual support for giving students a solid foundation for expository writing. The text includes examples of completed frameworks and paragraphs. Blank frameworks are included in the appendices. For assistance with narrative structure, teachers may wish to consult other texts (Westby 1991).

Classic Definition of a Paragraph

The basic *paragraph*—the rudimentary, typical framework used by teachers across the United States—begins with an indented topic sentence that expresses a main idea. The number of sentences that support the topic sentence varies, as does the level of detail. The final sentence is a conclusion.

A basic paragraph presents information in a clear, coherent manner. In expository writing, the writer needs to present ideas that are closely related and clearly linked from one sentence to the next. To form a basic paragraph, then, the writer must be able to:

- select a topic

- formulate a topic sentence

- sequence information logically

- support the topic with sufficient, relevant details

- use a verb tense consistently

- incorporate a variety of sentences

- employ transitional words to specify the relationships between sentences

- eliminate run-on sentences

- formulate a concluding sentence

Subroutines of Writing

Why is writing difficult for so many children, both with and without learning and language difficulties? Knowing the basic requirements of a paragraph does not ensure a coherent, reflective piece of writing. Many students need explicit, repeated practice to internalize the patterns of written language. They need to master subroutines of writing before they can meet the demands of factual writing. Once they can automatically perform the subroutines, they can attend to the content and coherence of the paragraph (Norris and Hoffman 1993). The subroutines include:

- producing legible handwriting at an acceptable pace

- retrieving words and formulating sentences efficiently

- following the rules of capitalization, punctuation, and spelling

- using metacognitive strategies (planning, monitoring, and problem-solving)

- employing metalinguistic awareness (knowledge of sound, word, sentence, and discourse structure)

The Value of Paragraph Frameworks

As students write, they need to monitor the subroutines of writing and remember the paragraph structure required for the assignment simultaneously. This places a heavy demand on working memory.

A *paragraph framework* is a visual display that acts like a structural blueprint. Lines and slots cue placement of the topic, supporting, and concluding sentences. *Mini-scaffolds* provide logical strategies for such skills as word retrieval and sentence formulation. An effective framework allows less-able readers and writers to see the explicit organization of a specific type of expository paragraph. It helps free up the mental energy students need to attend to the content and coherence of the paragraph. As the writer builds the information in each sentence, the framework holds it in place for reference. It enables the writer to track relevant information from one sentence to the next.

This chapter provides teaching strategies and frameworks for:

- object description paragraphs

- process paragraphs

- enumerative paragraphs

- comparison paragraphs

- contrast paragraphs

- comparison-contrast paragraphs

- brief essay paragraphs

Teachers should introduce students to the paragraph frameworks in the order listed above, as each framework relies on mastery of the one(s) preceding it.

Critical Roles of Brainstorming and Oral Rehearsal

Brainstorming, cueing, and classroom discussion are oral activities that not only allow students to hear how others think about the same topic, but also encourage them to evaluate and clarify their background knowledge. With a paragraph framework and teacher guidance, students can take turns orally rehearsing their ideas for a paragraph, one sentence at a time. The teacher models correct language use and clarifies incorrect information. The teacher also makes students explicitly aware of the relationship between spoken and written language structures.

The Object Description Paragraph Framework

A well-written expository paragraph relies on accurate facts and specific details. Once students master techniques for expanding simple sentences and the Easy Four Adjectives (color, size, shape, and number), teachers can introduce them to paragraphs that describe a familiar object. The *object description paragraph* focuses on the most salient parts of an object. An object description paragraph framework enables less-able writers to produce a cohesive result.

By focusing on a thematic unit, such as the Wild West, students gain a rich list of concrete nouns to describe. Teachers elicit names for an object's parts in logical order by having students visually scan the object from top to bottom or left to right. Teachers show students how to observe and analyze what they are looking at to determine its most significant aspects.

Each descriptive sentence in the paragraph is a kernel sentence expanded with adjectives. To produce an object description paragraph, teachers must enable students to:

- analyze an object thoughtfully and select its most salient features

- choose the most specific adjectives

- understand the function of the object's parts

- use visual-spatial organization to order the component parts of an object

The procedures below help students develop a topic sentence for an object description paragraph, provide accurate and precise descriptions in the body of the paragraph, and write a concluding sentence. Students use the object description paragraph framework as a worksheet. A sample follows on the facing page.

The Topic Sentence

A descriptive paragraph begins with a topic sentence that makes a statement about the object's general appearance. The topic sentence adheres to the structure below.

Article	Noun	Is/Are	Category	Who/ Which/That	General Appearance
The	coyote	is	a wild dog	that	looks like a German shepherd.

FRAMEWORK FOR OBJECT DESCRIPTION

Name: _____

Date: _____

Day: _____

Description of: _____*a coyote*_____

Topic Sentence: *A coyote* *is* *a mammal* *that* *looks like a German Shepherd.*

    Topic Noun + is/are + Category + who/which/that + General Appearance

Key Features: _*ears*_ , _*muzzle*_ , _*coat*_ , _*legs*_ , _*paws*_ , _*tail*_

Article	Adjective	Adjective	Noun	Function Verb
The	alert	triangular	ears	listen for danger.
A	sensitive	pointed	muzzle	sniffs for food.
A	thick	grayish	coat	protects it from the cold.
	strong	thin	legs	enable the coyote to chase prey.
The	padded	black	paws	travel silently across the prairie.
A	long	bushy	tail	acts as a signal flag.

Concluding Sentence: _*In conclusion, the coyote resembles a German shepherd and its unique features help it to survive.*_

The Body

The body of an object description paragraph relies on adjectives that describe salient parts of the object. The teacher directs students to write in the present tense unless the object is of historical interest (e.g., woolly mammoth and brontosaurus). Students make the paragraph coherent by spatially ordering the parts and choosing accurate adjectives. Students use synonyms to avoid repeating adjectives and function verbs. When students understand each part's function, they are better able to link the sentences.

First, the teacher shows students a colored picture, such as one that depicts a coyote. The teacher asks students to analyze the picture and brainstorm the coyote's features. The teacher writes students' words on the blackboard.

The teacher then asks students to identify the coyote's six most salient features from the list on the blackboard. Students number them according to the coyote's body structure, from left to right. (A top-to-bottom order is another option, especially if the coyote is sitting.) The teacher writes the number by each part, then rewrites the list in numerical order. Students write the key features in order in their frameworks, by the heading "Key Features." Students then copy the key features, in order, under the heading "Nouns." In this example, the nouns are body parts.

In a turn-taking format, the teacher assigns each student a body part to describe. The teacher reminds students to use precise words, a variety of adjectives and function verbs, and synonyms. Students' responses need to be logical and accurate.

The Concluding Sentence

When describing a single object or person, the concluding sentence is a general impression of the object that also reflects the significance of its particular parts. Teachers need to offer students strong support for this task, including guiding questions. Once students know complex sentence patterns and are more flexible with language, they begin to develop their own logical conclusions.

A concluding sentence in this sample paragraph might be: "In conclusion, the coyote resembles a German shepherd and its unique features help it to survive." A script for eliciting this sentence follows.

> **Teacher**: What would happen if the coyote didn't have these specific parts?
>
> **Student**: The coyote wouldn't be able to survive.

Teacher: That's right. Do these unique features help it to survive? Can you put this information into a concluding sentence?

Student: The coyote resembles a German shepherd and its unique features help it to survive.

Putting It Together

The teacher shows the class a colored picture of a prairie coyote. Students are familiar with this animal from class discussions about pioneer and Native American life on the prairie. The teacher instructs students to identify the coyote's most salient features.

Teacher: Please look carefully at the picture of the coyote so we can brainstorm the parts that we see. Let's start with you, Theresa. Bill's next, then Sam, and so on. I'll write your answers on the board as we go.

Theresa: Ears.

Bill: Nose.

Sam: Eyes.

Theresa: Hair.

Teacher: Theresa, when we refer to an animal's hair, we call it a different word, like in a lady's fur c-.

Theresa: Coat.

Bill: Whiskers.

Sam: Tail.

Teacher: You're getting many of the obvious parts, but we need to observe the coyote closely to identify additional significant features. As I point to various parts of the coyote's body, you tell me what each one is. (Points to legs.) Yes, those are legs. (Points to teeth.) And those are teeth. What are these? (Points to paws.) Yes, these are the paws. What are at the end of the paws? (Points to claws.) Yes, claws. What do we call this part of the coyote's face, which has the nose at the end and whiskers on the soft skin below? It's a two-syllable word that begins with *m* and rhymes with "puzzle." (Points to muzzle.) Yes, the word is muzzle. Now all of the coyote's significant features are on the board. We can only choose the six most important ones. Without these parts, the coyote would not have survived as long as he has. Let's put a check beside the six most important parts. We'll take turns again as you make your choices.

The class chooses legs, muzzle, paws, coat, tail, and ears.

Teacher: I agree that these are the most important features of the coyote. Now we need to number them according to the coyote's body structure. We'll use a left-to-right order because the coyote is standing.

As students take turns numbering the parts, the teacher writes the number beside each word. (There is more than one "right" order, since the focus is on developing a logical sequence of parts.) The teacher then rewrites the list in numerical order using a description paragraph framework on the blackboard. This makes it easy for students to copy. The ordered list is ears, muzzle, coat, legs, paws, and tail.

Teacher: Now you are ready to fill in your own paragraph framework. (Hands out an object description paragraph framework to each student) First of all, we need to think of a topic sentence that follows the outline on this worksheet. As you compose the sentence, I will write it in the framework on the blackboard. Sam, what are we describing and what is its category?

Sam: We are describing a coyote, and it is an animal.

Teacher: (Writes "A coyote is" on the blackboard, beside "Topic Sentence.") That's true, but let's be more specific. There are six animal types to choose from: mammal, bird, fish, reptile, amphibian, and insect. Is the coyote a reptile or an insect?

Sam: Of course not. A coyote is a mammal.

Teacher: (Writes "mammal" on the blackboard.) That's right, Sam. The coyote is a mammal. Is it a "who," "which," or "that"?

Sam: That . . . lives on the prairie in the West.

Teacher: That is a correct idea, but the topic sentence outline requires you to provide a general appearance response. Remember, the purpose of the topic sentence in an object description paragraph is to let the reader know that the paragraph is going to give an accurate physical description—in this case, of a coyote. What popular dog does the coyote look like?

Sam: A German shepherd.

Teacher: Yes, it certainly does, especially to the untrained eye. Now repeat the complete topic sentence.

Sam: A coyote is a mammal that looks like a German shepherd.

Teacher: (Writes "that looks like a German shepherd" on the blackboard.) Thank you, Sam. You did a fine job. Everyone may now copy the topic sentence. When you are finished, you may write the coyote's key features in order in the paragraph framework. Use the blanks after the heading "Key Features."

The teacher checks to ensure that each student has correctly copied the topic sentence into the framework.

Teacher: Now I want you to copy the key features in order into the paragraph framework. Put them under the heading "Nouns," which in this case are body parts of the coyote.

The teacher writes the key features under "Nouns" on the blackboard and checks students' papers.

Teacher: Now we're ready to describe a coyote. We'll use the turn-taking format. I'll assign each of you one or more body parts to describe. Remember to think of the most precise adjectives you can. You cannot repeat any adjectives or function verbs. You may use synonyms. Your responses need to be logical and accurate. OK, Bill, you're first. How do you describe the coyote's ears?

Bill: The pointed, triangular ears listen for danger.

Teacher: (Records Bill's response in the framework on the blackboard). That's a fine description, Bill. Can you think of a synonym for "pointed"? If the coyote's ears are up, he is the opposite of bored. I'm looking for a two-syllable word. A-.

Bill: Alert.

Teacher: (Erases "pointed" and writes "alert.") Terrific! Read your sentence back.

Bill: The alert, triangular ears listen for danger.

Teacher: You may copy this sentence into your paragraph frameworks.

The class describes each key feature of the coyote in this way. If necessary, the teacher reminds students that not every sentence needs to begin with an article. Size and number adjectives, for example, do not always require an article to precede them. (Grammar and mechanics are better taught in the context of sentence structure, however.)

Student's Paragraph Copied from the Object Description Framework

A Coyote

A coyote is a mammal that looks like a German Shepherd. The alert, triangular ears listen for danger. A sensitive, pointed muzzle sniffs for food. A thick, grayish coat protects it from the cold. Strong, thin legs enable the coyote to chase prey. The padded black paws travel silently across the prairie. A long, bushy tail acts as a signal flag. In conclusion, the coyote resembles a German shepherd and its unique features help it to survive.

The teacher then guides students to a coherent conclusion. The teacher writes it in the framework on the blackboard, and students copy it onto their paragraph frameworks.

Finally, the teacher asks for a volunteer to read the complete paragraph. A sample paragraph follows. If the student decides that it is an important piece of writing or potentially part of a short report, the teacher can instruct the class to rewrite the paragraph on lined paper.

The Process Paragraph Framework

The *process paragraph framework* outlines five steps—using the transitional words "first," "then," "next," "after that," and "finally"—to signal the specific parts of a process. This step-by-step format helps students explain how something is made. Teachers can reduce the number of steps when introducing the process paragraph to younger or less linguistically able students.

To help students order the steps for making or building something, the teacher encourages them to apply their background knowledge to thematic information, such as pioneer life. For example, the teacher can ask students to recall what they know about building a house, then to relate that knowledge to the pioneer's task of building a log cabin.

To write a process paragraph, students must be able to:

- analyze pictures or real-life experiences that depict specific processes (e.g., building a log cabin and making candles)

- engage in discussions about the specific processes for making things or achieving goals

- apply background knowledge and experience to what is less familiar

- select the most salient steps to complete a process

- order the steps into a process

The procedures below help students formulate a topic sentence for a process paragraph, provide the most salient and logical sequences in the body of the paragraph, and compose a concluding sentence. Students use the framework for a process paragraph as a guide. A sample follows on the next page.

The Topic Sentence

A process paragraph begins with a topic sentence that states how to make or accomplish something. Teachers can cue students toward the topic sentence with a guiding question. For example:

> **Teacher**: Did it take many steps to build a log cabin?

> **Student**: It took many steps to build a log cabin.

As teachers repeatedly model cues for topic sentences, students learn to formulate their own prompts.

The Body

To formulate the body of a process paragraph, students select the most important steps and place them in sequence. To free up mental energy for this analysis, students need to practice the transitional words—"first," "then," "next," "after that," and "finally"—until they can retrieve them automatically. Students should use synonyms to avoid repetition, especially

FRAMEWORK FOR PROCESS PARAGRAPH

Name: _____

Date: _____

Day: _____

Question: _____*Did it take many steps to build a log cabin?*_____

Topic Sentence:

(Restate the question) *It took many steps to build a log cabin.*_____

_____

First,   *First, the pioneers cut down the trees and cleared the land.*_____

_____

Why?/How? _____

Then,   *Then, they trimmed off the limbs and branches and prepared the shingles.*

Why?/How? _____

_____

Next,   *Next, some volunteers prepared the foundation once the land was ready.*

Why?/How? _____

_____

After that,   *After that, they put up the sides of the cabin and cut out a front doorway*

*and windows.*_____

Why?/How? _____

_____

Finally,   *Finally, the pioneers laid a roof and put up a chimney.*_____

_____

Why?/How? _____

_____

Concluding Sentence: *In conclusion, it was hard, dangerous work to build a log cabin, and*

*it took a long time.*_____

of subject nouns. Students should also write in the present tense unless the topic specifically requires the past (historical) or future (planning) tense. Students focus on the relevance of information, use precise vocabulary, and mindfully sequence the information to achieve coherence.

First, the teacher directs students to analyze a picture (such as pioneers building a log cabin in the western wilderness). The class brainstorms the steps to build a log cabin. The teacher writes the steps in a column on the left side of the blackboard.

As an oral exercise, the teacher asks students to select the five most important steps from the list and to order them logically using the transitional words "first," "then," "next," "after that," and "finally." The picture remains visible for reference. The teacher numbers the steps on the blackboard, and students rewrite them in order in their frameworks.

The teacher then explains that using the same noun—pioneers—as the subject in each step is repetitive and impairs the flow of the paragraph. The teacher asks students to think of synonyms for pioneers and writes the synonyms (including pronouns) in another column on the blackboard.

In a turn-taking format, the teacher asks students to compose the steps, starting with the word "first." The teacher reminds students to analyze the picture for accurate information and important details. The teacher writes each student's sentence on the blackboard. The student reads it back and makes changes if necessary. Here is a script for this lesson:

> **Teacher**: Let's look carefully at this picture of the pioneers raising a cabin. It's obvious that a lot of work was done before they could actually raise the log sides. (Reads a brief description that accompanies the picture that verifies her words.) Let's brainstorm the steps it took to build this log cabin. It may help if you think about a house you've seen being built in your neighborhood. Let's start with you, Sam, and then the next person will take a turn. I'll write your responses on the blackboard.
>
> **Sam**: They had to cut out the windows.
>
> **Bill**: The pioneers put up the sides of the cabin.
>
> **Teacher**: Bill, what did they have to do to the logs before they could use them?
>
> **Bill**: They trimmed off the limbs and branches.
>
> **Teacher**: (Points to the roof area in the photograph and cues for that step.)

Theresa: A roof was added.

Teacher: Yes, the roof would be put on as soon as possible. What is nailed to the roof so it won't leak, Theresa? (Pause.) It's a two-syllable word. Sh-.

Theresa: Shingles.

Teacher: Good, they had to prepare the shingles.

Sam: The pioneers cut down the trees and cleared the land.

Teacher: You have done a good job thinking of many of the important steps the pioneers needed to take to build a log cabin. I'm going to read a short passage from this book that gives a very precise explanation of what the pioneers had to do to prepare for a cabin-raising. (Reads, then asks if students learned any additional steps for their process paragraph. Shows the class a picture of a completed log cabin.)

Theresa: The pioneers needed a chimney and a front doorway.

Teacher: Good. I think those are the last important ideas we need before we organize our sequence, but I notice we have left out one of the very first steps. It was mentioned in the passage I read to you. Once the land was ready, the pioneers had to prepare the foundation. (Writes this step on the blackboard.) We can use all your ideas in our sequence, but we need to combine some of them into one sentence. Now I want you to put the steps in a logical order by matching them with one of the transitional words on the blackboard. I'll write the transitional word beside its step. OK, Bill, it's your turn.

Bill: Write the word "first" next to "cut down the trees and cleared the land."

Sam: I think the word "then" goes with "trimmed off the limbs and branches."

Theresa: The word "next" should go with "prepared the foundation."

Bill: I think "after that" goes with "put up the sides of the cabin."

Sam: The word "finally" goes with "cut out the windows."

Teacher: You've done a good job organizing the steps into a sequence. Let's take a look.

Transition Word	Step
First	Cut down the trees and cleared the land
Then	Trimmed off the limbs and branches
Next	Prepared the foundation
After that	Put up the sides of the cabin
Finally	Cut out the windows

Teacher: Four steps are not included: prepared the shingles, laid a roof, put up a chimney, and cut out a front doorway. From the reading, you learned that the shingles were prepared and split by hand. They had to be ready once the sides were up and the base of the roof was ready. Where do you think we could put that idea, Theresa?

Theresa: I think it could go with "trimmed off the limbs and branches" because that's when the pioneers would be working with the logs to get wood for building.

Teacher: Nicely analyzed! I'll write "prepared the shingles" beside "trimmed off the limbs and branches." Bill, look at the last three steps that are left. What are the very last steps the pioneers took to finish the cabin?

Bill: The word "finally" should go with "laid a roof and put up a chimney."

Teacher: I agree with you. (Writes "laid a roof and put up a chimney" beside "finally.") Sam, where in our sequence should we move "cut out the windows"? It's not the last step in the sequence any more. Look carefully at the photograph. The window has already been cut out before the wall is completely up.

Sam: Oh, I see what's happening. "Cut out the windows" can be added to "put up the sides of the cabin." Match "cut out the windows" with "after that."

Teacher: You are paying excellent attention to the details of this cabin-raising. Theresa, to which of our steps should we add "cut out a front doorway"? If a window was cut before the sides were completely up, then . . . (Points to the photograph.)

Theresa: A front doorway was cut as the sides of the cabin were put up. Write "cut out a front doorway" beside "after that."

Teacher: I think we're all set now. I'm going to write the final list on the blackboard and erase the old one.

Transition
Word   *Step*

First   Cut down the trees and cleared the land

Then   Trimmed off the limbs and branches and prepared the shingles

Next   Prepared the foundation

After that   Put up the sides of the cabin and cut out a front doorway and windows

Finally   Laid a roof and put up a chimney

Teacher: Now we need to think of synonyms for the word "pioneers." We know that repeating "pioneers" in each sentence doesn't make the paragraph flow smoothly.

The students suggest the synonyms "helpers," "men," "they," and "volunteers." The teacher writes them under the final list of steps.

Teacher: Now you are ready to fill in your own paragraph framework. Remember, please wait until I finish writing a sentence on the board before you copy it into your frameworks. Sometimes we'll make changes. (Hands out a process paragraph framework to each student) First of all, you need to create a topic sentence. Then you'll take turns orally composing the steps in the sequence. I'll fill in the paragraph framework on the blackboard, one sentence at a time, as each of you dictates your sentence to me. Sam, you begin by composing the topic sentence. Read the question and then make a statement from it.

Sam: Did it take many steps to build a log cabin? It took many steps to build a log cabin.

Teacher: (Writes this sentence on the blackboard, beside the heading "Topic Sentence.") Good. Theresa?

Theresa: First, the pioneers cut down the trees and cleared the land.

Teacher: Bill, you have two ideas to think about. Combine them into one sentence.

Bill: Then, they trimmed off the limbs and branches and prepared the shingles.

Sam: Next, some volunteers prepared the foundation.

In this way, the teacher breaks the process down into logical steps. The teacher facilitates discussion by reminding students to think about what they know about the topic, as well as how the sentence structures they are learning can help them express what they mean to say. Students who are still learning the expanded kernel sentence need to work with fewer steps and a manageable number of details.

The Concluding Sentence

The concluding sentence is an overall impression of the effort involved to complete the process. Weak writers need extensive scaffolding or support to form this impression. An effective method is for the teacher to pose questions that generate supplemental information, then ask students to synthesize a conclusion.

> **Teacher**: Did the pioneers have a difficult time building the log cabin?
>
> **Student**: Yes, it took a lot of hard work.
>
> **Teacher**: Yes, it was very hard work—and dangerous, too. There were many accidents cutting down those big trees and rolling the logs around. It also took a long time before the cabin was finished. Can you put this information into a concluding sentence?
>
> **Student**: It was hard, dangerous work to build a log cabin and it took a long time.

Teachers need to provide strong support for students to develop a conclusion that is coherent with the rest of the paragraph. With practice, students recognize the logic of the teacher's guiding questions and to avoid simple responses that are not unified with the paragraph.

A sample of the completed paragraph follows on the next page.

Elaborating on a Process Paragraph

Over time, students accumulate a lot of information about the selected theme and refine their writing skills for process paragraphs. Once students master the transitional words in order and can closely link the steps into action sequences, they are ready to elaborate the steps with inferences.

The teacher asks each student to select a step and explain why it took place. Students call on their knowledge and, with practice and guidance, make inferences. Eventually students can use this strategy independently to add information to a step. The teacher can also help students elaborate

Student's Paragraph Copied from the Process Framework

Building a Log Cabin

It took many steps to build a log cabin. First, the pioneers cut down the trees and cleared the land. Then, they trimmed off the limbs and branches and prepared shingles. Next, some volunteers prepared the foundation once the land was ready. After that, they put up the sides of the cabin and cut out a front doorway and windows. Finally, the pioneers laid a roof and put up a chimney. In conclusion, it was hard, dangerous work to build a log cabin, and it took a long time.

on information by asking what difference it makes that a particular step was taken. These two questions help students add relevant, precise details to the body of a process paragraph.

Teacher: We are going to add information to each of the steps by asking *why*. Theresa, read the first step out loud, please.

Theresa: First the pioneers cut down the trees and cleared the land.

Teacher: Fine. Why did the pioneers have to clear the land? Remember not to begin your sentence with "because." Hold that word and dictate the rest of your answer to me. I'll write your response on the blackboard.

Theresa: They needed the lumber and the space to put the log cabin on.

Teacher: Yes, it would have been difficult to build a cabin among the trees. Bill, let's see if you can think of a *how* response. How would it have made a difference if the pioneers hadn't cut down the trees and cleared the land?

Bill: It would have been impossible to build a log cabin in the middle of all those trees.

Teacher: Yes, it certainly would have been impossible. Bill, read the first step and the sentences that elaborate on it. Let's see if all the ideas fit nicely.

Bill: First the pioneers cut down the trees and cleared the land. They needed a space to build the log cabin. It would have been impossible to build a log cabin in the middle of all those trees.

Teacher: Thank you, Bill. I like the way those sentences go together, don't you? Sam, read the next step and provide a *why* response. Remember not to begin your sentence with "because."

Sam: Then they trimmed off the limbs and branches and had to prepare the shingles. The pioneers needed smooth logs to build with and . . .

Teacher: Once the roof was on, the shingles were put on as soon as possible.

Sam: The shingles were put on as soon as the roof was on.

Teacher: Sam, you did a nice job paraphrasing my information. Let's provide one more *why* response to finish the paragraph.

Once students practice cause-and-effect reasoning (*why* information) for two or three steps, the teacher asks them to elaborate on all the steps. As they work, the teacher can occasionally ask them a *how* question about a particular step. Teachers gradually ask students to elaborate each step with a *how* response in addition to the cause-and-effect reasoning. These strategies for developing inferences help students write a process paragraph with sufficient, relevant details.

The Enumerative Paragraph Framework

Effective expository writing includes specific examples that clarify meaning. The *enumerative paragraph framework* accomplishes this expository goal. The topic sentence of an enumerative paragraph makes a general statement. The body consists of three examples that relate to and support the topic sentence. The transitions "first of all," "secondly," and "thirdly" mark the examples. The factual details of each example are flagged with the word "fact" and form complete sentences. The examples' detail and relevance make the paragraph effective (Fawcett and Sandberg 1988).

For students to write an enumerative paragraph, they must be able to:

- engage in discussions about an assigned topic and intellectually process information for relevance and accuracy

- categorize information (e.g., generate a list of items in a category)

- associate specific examples and salient facts with a given piece of information

Teachers can help students develop a topic sentence for an enumerative paragraph, provide specific examples and well-chosen facts in the body of the paragraph, and compose a concluding sentence by following the procedures below. These procedures are for use with the enumerative paragraph framework. A sample follows on the facing page.

The Topic Sentence

An enumerative paragraph begins with a topic sentence that makes a general statement and needs specific examples to support it. Teachers can cue for the topic sentence with a theme-centered question.

Teacher: Do many wild animals live on the prairie?

Student: Many wild animals live on the prairie.

Repeated cueing by the teacher prepares students to self-cue for a topic sentence.

The Body

The body of an enumerative paragraph offers specific examples that explain the general topic. Students memorize "first of all," "secondly," and "thirdly" as cues for three examples. Once students can supply examples, the teacher asks them to add meaningful facts. Students write in the present tense unless the topic is of historical interest (past tense) or related to planning (future tense).

In the instructions that follow, the theme is animal life of the western prairie. The assumption is that the class has studied the theme and generated both object description and process paragraphs. Books about the

FRAMEWORK FOR ENUMERATIVE PARAGRAPH

Name: _____

Date: _____

Day: _____

Question: *Are there many wild animals that live on the prairie?* _____

_____

Topic Sentence:

(Restate the question) *There are many wild animals that live on the prairie.* _____

_____

First of all, *First of all, the prairie dogs live in prairie dog towns.* _____

_____

Fact: *They whistle when there is danger.* _____

_____

Secondly, *Secondly, rattlesnakes like to hunt the prairie dogs.* _____

_____

Fact: *The rattlesnakes crawl into the prairie dog tunnels and trap them.* _____

_____

Thirdly, *Thirdly, the buffaloes like to visit the prairie dog towns.* _____

_____

Fact: *They roll in the dust, but they don't hurt the prairie dogs.* _____

_____

Concluding Sentence: *In conclusion, these wild animals have adapted well to this* _____

environment. _____

western prairie are on display, and animal pictures hang on the wall. The teacher has written the enumerative paragraph framework on the blackboard and prepared worksheets for the class.

First, the teacher shows the class several theme-centered, colored pictures of animal life on the western prairie. The teacher asks students to brainstorm a list of the animals they see. Students can also name prairie animals not in the pictures.

One at a time, students name the animals. The teacher lists them on the left side of the blackboard. After the class generates a substantial list, the teacher asks students to categorize each animal as a mammal, bird, or reptile. In a turn-taking format, each student reads a word (with the teacher's help, if necessary) and identifies its category.

Next, the teacher calls on students to choose animals from the list and compose sentences that begin with "first of all," "secondly," and "thirdly." The teacher writes the sentences in the paragraph framework on the blackboard. The teacher reminds students not to copy the sentences onto their worksheets until each sentence is complete and correct.

Once students generate the three examples, the teacher asks them to add a fact to make each example more meaningful. In a turn-taking format, the teacher calls on students to compose fact sentences. The teacher writes each fact sentence below the example it supports. Students reread their sentences for accuracy and clarity.

The Concluding Sentence

The conclusion of an enumerative paragraph is the overall impression left by the examples and facts that support the topic sentence. Students need a reliable strategy for writing the concluding sentence, as the task requires them to synthesize a lot of factual detail. The teacher can model a concluding sentence pattern and ask students to paraphrase it.

> **Teacher**: We have talked about the prairie dog, the rattlesnake, and the buffaloes that live on the prairie. What makes it possible for them to live in the same area?
>
> **Student**: We know that the rattlesnake hunts prairie dogs and the prairie dogs dig tunnels to hide.
>
> **Teacher**: That's true. Why do buffaloes like to visit the prairie dog towns?
>
> **Student**: Buffaloes like to roll in the dirt that the prairie dogs dig up. When buffaloes are there, the snakes stay away.

Teacher: Have these wild animals adapted well to their environment? Can you put this information into a concluding sentence?

Student: These wild animals have adapted well to their environment.

After repeated practice, students internalize this cueing and apply it independently.

Putting It Together

The teacher holds up a book with colored pictures of animals that live on the prairie. As students look at the pictures, the teacher asks them to brainstorm a list of animals.

Teacher: You have learned a lot about the animals that live on the prairie. Let's see how many of them you can name. I'll write your answers on the blackboard. Let's start with you, Sam. Then Theresa and Bill can have a turn.

Sam: I see a prairie dog.

Theresa: There's a coyote.

Bill: I know what that tall, brown animal is. You said it was a kind of deer.

Teacher: I like the way you are cueing yourself, Bill. The word you're thinking of has one syllable and its first sound is "e-."

Bill: Oh, now I know. Elk. The animal is an elk.

The students continue to name animals.

Teacher: We have enough animals listed on the blackboard. Each of you will choose the animal you want to use in a sentence. Now you are ready to fill in your own paragraph framework. (Hands out enumerative paragraph frameworks.) First of all, we need to think of a topic sentence, which requires you to make a statement from a question. Do many wild animals live on the prairie? Copy that question into your frameworks. (Waits until students finish.) Who will compose the topic sentence from the question? I will write it on the board. (Sam raises his hand.)

Sam: Many wild animals live on the prairie.

Teacher: That's a nice topic sentence, Sam. (Writes the sentence on the blackboard.) All of you may copy the topic sentence. (Checks each paper.) On your frameworks, you need to use the words "first of all," "secondly," and "thirdly." These words let the reader know that you are listing three specific examples of something—in this case, animals that live on the prairie. Your sentences need to begin with one of these words. OK, Theresa, why don't you create the first example? I'll write it beside "first of all," which signals the first example. Which animal are you going to choose? Don't forget to read your sentence back and make any corrections before everyone copies it.

Theresa: I choose "prairie dogs." First of all, the prairie dogs live in prairie dog towns.

Teacher: I like what you said about prairie dogs. I'm sure a lot of people don't know they live in towns. It's your turn, Bill. What's your word?

Bill: I'm choosing "coyotes." Secondly, coyotes like to hunt the jack rabbits.

Sam: My word is "buffaloes." Thirdly, the buffaloes graze on the prairie grass.

Teacher: You have all given good examples. Now we need to think of a fact that relates to each example. It will help if you read your example before you compose a fact sentence. I'll write each of your facts on the blackboard. Theresa, it's your turn.

Theresa: First of all, the prairie dogs live in prairie dog towns. They whistle when there is danger.

Bill: Secondly, coyotes like to hunt jack rabbits. The jack rabbits jump high and the coyotes pounce on them.

Sam: Thirdly, the buffaloes graze on the prairie grass. They like to visit prairie dog towns and roll in the dust.

Teacher: You have all done a fine job expressing yourselves. You know a lot about the animals, don't you? It's easier to think of things to say when you are familiar with the facts. Now we have to think of a concluding sentence.

Students need scaffolding to formulate the concluding sentence. An effective method is for teachers to ask questions and provide supplemental information, then invite students to synthesize conclusions.

Teacher: We've talked about prairie dogs, coyotes, and buffaloes. What makes it possible for them to live in the same area?

Student: They eat different food.

Teacher: That's right. These animals share the same environment, but they use it in different ways. Have they adjusted well to their environment? Can you think of a way to say this in your own words?

Student: In conclusion, prairie dogs, coyotes, and buffaloes use the land in different ways, and they have adjusted well to their environment.

A sample of the finished enumerative paragraph follows.

Student's Paragraph Copied from Enumerative Framework

Wild Animals of the Prairie

There are many wild animals that live on the prairie. First of all, the prairie dogs live in prairie dog towns. They whistle when there is danger. Secondly, rattlesnakes like to hunt the prairie dogs. The rattlesnakes crawl into the prairie dog tunnels and trap them. Thirdly, the buffaloes like to visit the prairie dog towns. They roll in the dust, but they don't hurt the prairie dogs. In conclusion, these wild animals have adapted well to their environment.

Expository Paragraph Frameworks

The Comparison Paragraph Framework

The *comparison paragraph* focuses on the similarities between two concrete nouns in the same category. It requires students to recognize salient features common to a pair of concrete nouns, as well as less significant attributes. In the animal category, information may include hunting habits or rearing of the young.

Students need to think about two objects simultaneously and recognize shared characteristics. This places a heavy demand on working memory. Therefore, it is important for students to focus on relevant facts. Focusing students' attention is easier when the language lesson incorporates familiar thematic content.

The framework for a comparison paragraph outlines three comparison sentences. The sentences are numbered. Comparisons are marked with the transitional words "both," "each," and "like." While any of the comparisons can come first, if the paragraph includes both physical features and less visible features, the physical features should come first.

To compose three sentences for a comparison paragraph, students must be able to:

- engage in discussions about an assigned topic and intellectually process information for relevance and accuracy

- categorize information (e.g., common characteristics shared by two concrete nouns in the same category)

- think of subtle similarities, which requires a deeper understanding of the concrete nouns they are comparing

- use the transitional words "both," "each," and "like" to mark comparisons

The procedures below help students develop a topic sentence for a comparison paragraph, provide specific points of comparison in the body of the paragraph, and compose a concluding sentence. The procedures are for use with the comparison paragraph framework. A sample follows on the facing page.

FRAMEWORK FOR COMPARISON PARAGRAPH

Name: _____

Date: _____

Day: _____

Comparison of: _____*coyote*_____ and _____*prairie fox*_____

Synonyms	Similarities
wild dogs	1. *grayish red fur*
carnivores	2. *bushy tail*
they	3. *hunt rodents*

Question: *Are the coyote and the prairie fox similar in many ways?*

Topic Sentence: *The coyote and the prairie fox are similar in many ways.*
       (Restate the question)

1. *Both the coyote and the prairie fox have grayish red fur.*

2. *Each of the wild dogs has a bushy tail.*

3. *Like the coyote, the prairie fox hunts rodents.*

Concluding Sentence: *In conclusion, the coyote and the prairie fox look almost the same and they share the same environment.*

both   each   like

The Topic Sentence

The topic sentence in a comparison paragraph compares two concrete nouns in the same category. Students generate the topic sentence from a question, which the teacher writes on the blackboard. Students copy the question from the board, then compose the topic sentence. For example:

Question: Are the coyote and the prairie fox similar?

Topic sentence: The coyote and the prairie fox are similar in many ways.

The Body

The body of the paragraph consists of three comparison sentences about the topic. Students should first master the transitional words "both," "each," and "like" as a memory aid. Students then create a coherent paragraph by focusing on accuracy, using synonyms for the subject noun, and employing precise vocabulary. They write in the present tense. Weaker students require extensive practice and scaffolding to use formal language to make comparisons.

First, the teacher writes the comparison paragraph framework on the blackboard. The teacher then holds up colored pictures of a coyote and a prairie fox. The teacher asks students to name the animals they see, then writes "coyote" and "prairie fox" in the framework on the blackboard. Students copy the words onto their frameworks after the words "Comparison of."

The teacher next asks students to look at the physical characteristics of the animals and brainstorm the ways in which they are alike. The teacher writes students' responses on the left side of the blackboard.

After students generate a list of similarities, the teacher asks them to select three. The teacher then helps students put the three similarities in order for the paragraph and numbers them on the blackboard. Students copy the three similarities onto their frameworks in the box labeled "Similarities."

The teacher then asks students to think of synonyms for the nouns (coyote and prairie fox). Students volunteer "wild dogs," "carnivores," and "they." The teacher writes these words on the blackboard. Students copy the words in the box labeled "Synonyms."

The teacher assigns the first comparison to a student. The student chooses one of the transitional words—"both," "each," or "like"—to begin the sentence. The teacher writes the word after the number *1* on the framework.

The student then composes a sentence, and the teacher acts as a scribe. The student reads the sentence back and makes adjustments until it is correct. The rest of the class then copies the sentence onto their frameworks. The class repeats this process for the second and third comparisons.

The Concluding Sentence

The concluding sentence is a paraphrase of the topic sentence and may synthesize the factual details of the comparisons. Scaffolding helps students form a concluding sentence that reflects the characteristics shared by the compared objects.

> **Teacher**: We have talked about how the coyote and the prairie fox are similar. Why do they have these particular body parts?
>
> **Student**: They couldn't live without them.
>
> **Teacher**: That's true. Why are their fur coats grayish-red?
>
> **Student**: It's for camouflage. They can hide from their enemies.
>
> **Teacher**: Right. Their grayish-red fur blends in with the colors of the prairie. Both the coyote and the prairie fox hunt rodents in the same area. Won't they eat them all up?
>
> **Student**: No, because the coyote hunts mostly jack rabbits and the prairie fox hunts small rodents like mice.
>
> **Teacher**: Good. You really know your facts. They both hunt rodents, but they don't eat the same ones, do they? Each of these animals is very shy, so they stay out of each other's way. When animals share a common habitat, we say that they have adapted well to their environment. Can you restate this?
>
> **Student**: The coyote and the prairie fox have similar characteristics and they have adapted well to their environment.

Putting It Together

The teacher holds up colored pictures of a coyote and a prairie fox and asks students to think about the ways in which they are the same.

> **Teacher**: You are familiar with the coyote and the prairie fox. I want you to think about how they are the same and compare their common characteristics. I'll write your answers on the black-

board. Let's start with you, Bill. Then Sam and Theresa can have their turns.

Bill: They have grayish-red fur.

Sam: They both have a bushy tail.

Theresa: The coyote has pointed ears like the prairie fox.

Teacher: (Writes the responses on the blackboard.) You're doing a good job thinking about how the animals look the same. Let's think of other ways they are the same, such as the way they hunt.

Bill: I know. The coyote hunts jack rabbits and the prairie fox hunts mice.

Teacher: That's right. What is the category for jack rabbits and mice, Bill?

Bill: Rodents.

Teacher: Good. What do both animals do?

Bill: Both animals hunt rodents.

Teacher: (Writes Bill's response on the blackboard.) Sam, do you remember how the coyote and the prairie fox raise their pups? Are they part of a large pack, or do they form single-family units?

Sam: They form single-family units.

Teacher: Start your sentence with the word "both," Sam.

Sam: Both form single-family units.

Teacher: (Writes Sam's response on the blackboard.) You have thought of many ways that these animals are the same. Let's choose three comparisons, including one that's not so obvious. I'll number them and write them in the framework in the box labeled "Similarities." We'll do physical characteristics first.

The students choose, in order, "grayish-red fur," "bushy tail," and "hunt rodents." The teacher writes these similarities in the framework on the blackboard.

Teacher: OK, now you are ready to fill in your own paragraph framework. (Hands out a paragraph framework to each student.) First of all, you need to think of a topic sentence, which requires you to make a statement from a question. Here's the question: Are the coyote and the prairie fox similar? As you compose the sentence, I will write it in the framework on the blackboard. Who wants to compose the topic sentence? (Bill raises his hand.)

Bill: The coyote and the prairie fox are similar in many ways.

Teacher: Thank you, Bill. (Writes it on the blackboard.) All of you may copy the topic sentence. Then copy the three comparisons in the box labeled "Similarities." When you're finished, put your pencils down. (Pauses while students write.) OK, now we're ready to think of synonyms or pronouns for the nouns "coyote" and "prairie fox." We know that repeating the same words as the subject of the sentence is uninteresting and prevents the paragraph from flowing smoothly.

Students offer the synonyms "wild dogs," "carnivores," and "they." The teacher writes them in the box labeled "Synonyms." Students copy the words into their frameworks. The teacher checks students' work.

Teacher: Now we are ready to compose the comparison sentences. Theresa, choose one of the words at the bottom of the paragraph framework—"both," "each," or "like." Then use the first comparison to compose a sentence. I'll write it down as you say it.

Theresa: Both the coyote and the prairie fox have grayish-red fur.

Theresa reads the sentence back. The teacher praises her for her good work and writes the sentence on the blackboard. The class copies the sentence into their frameworks. Sam takes on the second comparison.

Sam: Each the coyote and the prairie fox have a bushy tail.

Teacher: Sam, read your sentence. Does it sound right?

Sam: No, but I don't know why.

Teacher: The word "each" combines with the subject differently than the word "both." Use the synonym "wild dogs" and compose the sentence.

Sam: Each the wild dog . . . (Realizes this doesn't sound right and starts again.) Each of the wild dogs have . . .

Teacher: The word "each" requires the verb "has," Sam.

Sam: Each of the wild dogs has a bushy tail.

Sam reads the sentence back. The teacher writes the sentence on the blackboard, and the class copies the sentence into their frameworks. Bill takes on the third comparison.

Bill: Like the coyote and the prairie dog, they hunt rodents.

Teacher: That's a good try, Bill, but we have to rephrase the sentence. Let's omit the words "and" and "they." We'll also add an *s* to "hunt" to say "hunts." I'll write as you say the sentence.

Bill: Like the coyote, the prairie fox hunts rodents.

Bill reads the sentence back. The teacher writes the sentence on the blackboard, and the class copies the sentence into their frameworks.

Teacher: Nice job, all of you. We'll continue to practice these sentence patterns until you can compose them without my help. Now we'll think of a concluding sentence that states that these animals are similar or share the same environment. Do the coyote and the prairie fox look somewhat the same? Do they share the same environment?

Bill: The coyote and the prairie fox look almost the same, and they share the same environment.

A sample of the finished paragraph follows.

Student's Paragraph Copied from Comparison Framework

The Coyote and the Prairie Fox

The coyote and the prairie fox are similar in many ways. Both the coyote and the prairie fox have grayish red fur. Each of the wild dogs has a bushy tail. Like the coyote, the prairie fox hunts rodents. In conclusion, the coyote and the prairie fox look almost the same and they share the same environment.

Elaborating on a Comparison Paragraph

Once students master the transitional words for a comparison paragraph and can compose comparison sentences, they are ready to elaborate on the sentences with a fact. Teachers can modify the framework for this task by adding a space after each comparison with the heading "Fact."

> **Teacher**: You have made good comparisons between the coyote and the prairie fox. We can add more information to our paragraph by adding facts that relate to each comparison. It is helpful to read your sentence before you think of a fact to add. Sam, it's your turn.

> **Sam**: Both the coyote and the prairie fox have grayish-red fur. The color is like camouflage and protects them from their enemies.

> **Theresa**: Each of the wild dogs has a bushy tail. (Pauses.)

> **Teacher**: The tail acts as a signal flag. When dogs wag their tails they are fr-. When their tails are way down, they are sc-.

> **Theresa**: Friendly and scared.

> **Teacher**: What kind of words are "friendly" and "scared"?

> **Theresa**: Those are inner-feelings words. Oh, I know. The tail signals how they feel.

> **Teacher**: Great. Bill?

> **Bill**: Like the coyote, the prairie fox hunts rodents. The coyote hunts jack rabbits, and the prairie fox hunts mice.

> **Teacher**: Good ideas, Bill, but you've used the word "hunts" three times. What synonyms can you think of so you don't repeat the word?

> **Bill**: The coyote chases jack rabbits and the prairie fox kills mice.

> **Teacher**: You have learned a lot about these animals. You didn't have much difficulty thinking of things to say.

The Contrast Paragraph Framework

A *contrast paragraph* focuses on the salient differences between two concrete nouns in the same category. As in the comparison paragraph, students analyze the nouns for physical and less discernible characteristics. The contrast paragraph framework consists of three contrast sentences. Contrasts are marked with the transitional words "but," "yet," and "however." While any of the contrasting ideas can come first, it is logical to contrast physical features before those less discernible when both are included.

To compose three sentences for a contrast paragraph, students must be able to:

- engage in discussions about an assigned topic and intellectually process information for relevance and accuracy

- categorize information (e.g., the differences between two concrete nouns in the same category)

- think of subtle differences, which requires a deeper understanding of the concrete nouns they are contrasting

- use the transitional words "but," "yet," and "however" to signal a contrast

The procedures below help students develop a topic sentence for a contrast paragraph, provide specific contrasts in the body of the paragraph, and compose a concluding sentence. These procedures are for use with the contrast paragraph framework. A sample follows on the facing page.

The Topic Sentence

The topic sentence contrasts two concrete nouns within the same category. Students generate the topic sentence from a question, which the teacher writes on the blackboard. Students copy the topic question from the board, then compose the topic sentence. For example:

> **Question**: Are the coyote and the prairie fox different?
>
> **Topic sentence:** The coyote and the prairie fox are different in many ways.

The Body

The body of the paragraph consists of three contrast sentences about the topic. Students should first master the transitional words "but," "yet," and "however" as a memory aid. Students then create a coherent paragraph by focusing on accuracy and using precise vocabulary. They write in the present tense. Weaker students require extensive practice and scaffolding to use formal language to make contrasts.

The paragraphs below offer detailed instruction. The instructions assume that the teacher has written the contrast paragraph framework on the

FRAMEWORK FOR CONTRAST PARAGRAPH

Name: _____

Date: _____

Day: _____

Contrast of: _____*coyote*_____ and _____*prairie fox*_____

Characteristics

Differences		Differences
1. *plain*	← muzzle →	1. *black smudge*
2. *long, thick*	← coat →	2. *short*
3. *pounces on the jack rabbit*	← hunting style →	3. *zigzags after the mice*

Question: *Are the coyote and the prairie fox different in many ways?*

Topic Sentence: *The coyote and the prairie fox are different in many ways.*
       (Restate the question)

1. *The coyote has a plain muzzle, but the prairie fox has a black smudge on his muzzle.*

2. *The coyote possesses a long, thick coat, yet the prairie fox has a short coat.*

3. *The coyote pounces on the jack rabbit; however, the prairie fox zigzags after the mice.*

Concluding Sentence: *In conclusion, the coyote and the prairie fox appear to be similar at first, but they are quite different.*

but   **yet**   **however**

blackboard, distributed the contrast paragraph framework as a worksheet to students, and helped students write the topic sentence.

First, the teacher displays colored pictures of a coyote and a prairie fox and asks students to name the animals they see. The teacher writes "coyote" and "prairie fox" in the framework on the blackboard. Students copy the words onto their frameworks, beside the words "Contrast of."

The teacher points to physical features the animals share and asks students to identify obvious differences between them. The teacher then encourages students to identify less discernible differences, such as hunting styles and food needs. The teacher may need to be more directive for students to identify the less dramatic differences. The class generates a list of three differing characteristics between the two animals. The teacher writes them in the framework on the blackboard, under the heading "Characteristics." The list starts with the physical differences and proceeds to less discernible differences. Students copy the three characteristics onto their frameworks.

Then, one at a time, the teacher asks students to articulate the difference between the two animals for each characteristic. The teacher writes students' answers for each animal in the appropriate box labeled "Differences" on the blackboard. Students copy the information onto their frameworks.

The next step is for students to compose the three contrast sentences orally. The teacher asks the class to select a transitional word—"but," "yet," or "however"—then writes the word outside the framework on the blackboard. The teacher then invites a student to use this word in a sentence that contrasts the coyote and the prairie fox. The teacher writes the student's sentence in the framework. The student reads the sentence back to make certain the contrast is correct, then the class copies the sentence onto their frameworks. The class follows the same procedure for the second and third sentences. The teacher reminds students to use synonyms for the verbs to avoid repetition.

The Concluding Sentence

The concluding sentence paraphrases the topic sentence and summarizes the overall impression left by the contrasting characteristics. Scaffolding helps students synthesize the factual details behind the contrast, which is essential to an effective conclusion.

> **Teacher**: We have explained how the coyote and the prairie fox are different in certain ways. They appear to be similar when you first look at them, don't they? They really are quite different after you learn about them. Can you say this in your own words?

Student: In conclusion, the coyote and the prairie fox appear to be similar at first, but they are quite different.

Putting It Together

The teacher hands out contrast paragraph frameworks. Students copy the question from the blackboard and restate it as a topic sentence. The teacher holds up colored pictures of a coyote and a prairie fox.

Teacher: What are the names of these animals, Bill?

Bill: A coyote and a prairie fox.

Teacher: That's right. I'll write the words "coyote" and "prairie fox" in the framework on the blackboard. You copy them. In an earlier lesson, you wrote a comparison paragraph about these animals, so you know how they are alike. Now I want you to focus on how they are different. We'll analyze some of their features to see the differences. Theresa, let's start with you. Take a close look at where I am pointing. What is this part called?

Theresa: That's a muzzle.

Teacher: Good. Sam, what's this part of the prairie fox called?

Sam: Coat.

Teacher: OK. Those are two features that we can easily analyze, so we'll use them. (Writes "muzzle" and "coat" under the heading "Characteristics.") Copy these words into your frameworks. Bill, we have examined two obvious differences, so let's think about something that's less obvious, such as hunting styles. How do the coyote and the prairie fox hunt?

Bill: The coyote pounces on jack rabbits, and the prairie fox zigzags to catch mice.

Teacher: I like that idea, so let's use it for our third difference. These animals seem to have a lot more in common than they do differences, don't they? What about size, Theresa?

Theresa: The coyote is bigger than the prairie fox.

Teacher: That's true. Which of these differences, hunting style or size, do you want to talk about? (Writes "hunting style," which the class chooses, as the third idea under "Characteristics." Students copy this down.) Sam, look at the muzzle of the coyote and then look at the muzzle of the prairie fox. How are they different?

Sam: The coyote doesn't have anything on his muzzle, but the prairie fox has a black mark.

Teacher: That's fine. If there isn't any marking on the muzzle, we say it's a plain muzzle. The black mark is called a smudge. Using this information, can you tell me how the coyote and the prairie fox are different?

Sam: The coyote has a plain muzzle and the prairie fox has a black smudge on his muzzle.

Teacher: Good work, Sam. (Writes "plain" in the box marked "Differences" for the coyote and "black smudge" under "Differences" for the prairie fox.) Copy these words onto your frameworks. Then we'll do the same for the next characteristic. Bill, it's your turn to tell us what's different about the coats of these animals.

Bill: Well, the coyote has longer and thicker fur, and the fur on the prairie fox is shorter.

Teacher: (Writes "long, thick" for the coyote and "short" for the prairie fox.) That's an accurate observation, Bill. Theresa, how are the hunting styles of the coyote and the prairie fox different?

Theresa: The coyote pounces on the jack rabbits, and the prairie fox zigzags after the mice.

Teacher: You have remembered some good facts. (Writes "pounces on jack rabbits" for the coyote and "zigzags after mice" for the prairie fox.) We have our three differences and the order in which we will write about them. Sam, will you please compose the first contrast sentence? Choose one word that marks contrast from the list at the bottom of the framework and combine it with the first idea that contrasts the coyote with the prairie fox.

Sam: I'm choosing "but" to combine the ideas. The coyote has a plain muzzle, but the prairie fox has a black smudge on his muzzle.

Teacher: (Writes the first sentence.) Good job, Sam. Now read it back to make sure it's correct. (The class copies the sentence after Sam rereads and approves it.) Bill, you compose the next contrast. Which word that marks contrast will you choose, "yet" or "however"?

Bill: I'm choosing "yet." The coyote has long, thick fur . . . I mean a long, thick coat, yet the prairie fox has a short coat. (Reads the sentence back.)

Teacher: Bill, can we use a synonym for the verb "has," such as "possesses" or "displays," so we don't overuse it?

Bill: Sure. The coyote has a long, thick coat, yet the prairie fox possesses a short coat. (Reads the sentence back. The class copies it.)

Teacher: These are great contrasting sentences. Theresa, it's your turn. Your word to mark a contrast is "however."

Theresa: The coyote pounces on the jack rabbit; however, the prairie fox zigzags after the mice. (Rereads her sentence. The class copies it.)

Teacher: You have learned a lot about these animals. You didn't have much difficulty thinking of things to say. Let's think of a concluding sentence. We know that the coyote and prairie fox have physical differences and also hunt differently. Who can say this and not use the same words I did?

Theresa: In conclusion, the coyote and the prairie fox don't look exactly the same, and they use different ways to hunt.

Teachers need to support students in developing a concluding sentence that conveys the ideas of the contrast and does not repeat the topic sentence. The conclusion of a contrast paragraph reflects the differences between two objects. It is important to emphasize that related objects may appear to be the same but differ in certain ways. The differences are not always easily observed.

A sample of the finished contrast paragraph follows on the next page.

Elaborating on a Contrast Paragraph

Once students master the contrast words and can use them to compose contrast sentences, they are ready to elaborate on the sentences with a fact. Teachers can modify the framework for this task by adding a space after each contrast with the heading "Fact."

Teacher: You have thought of important differences between the coyote and the prairie fox. We can add more information to our paragraph by adding facts that relate to each contrast. It will be helpful for you to read your sentence before you think of a fact to add. Bill, it's your turn.

Bill: The coyote has a plain muzzle, but the prairie fox has a black smudge on his muzzle. I'm not sure why the fox has the black smudge.

Student's Paragraph Copied from Contrast Framework

The Coyote and the Prairie Fox

The coyote and the prairie fox are different in many ways. The coyote has a plain muzzle, but the prairie fox has a black smudge on his muzzle. The coyote possesses a long, thick coat, yet the prairie fox has a short coat. The coyote pounces on the jack rabbit; however, the prairie fox zigzags after the mice. In conclusion, the coyote and the prairie fox appear to be similar at first, but they are quite different.

Teacher: You know the prairie fox is hunted by the coyote. Its grayish-red fur helps the fox hide in the prairie grass. The black smudge may act like a shadow when it's hiding. Can you put this idea into a sentence?

Bill: The black smudge may help the prairie fox hide from the coyote in the tall grass.

Teacher: Great. Theresa?

Theresa: The coyote has a long, thick coat, yet the prairie fox has a short coat. The fox is much smaller, but it has enough fur to keep it warm.

Teacher: Good work. Sam?

Sam: The coyote pounces on the jack rabbit; however, the prairie fox zigzags after the mice. The coyote grabs the jack rabbit as it bounces up while the prairie fox tracks the mice, which never travel in a straight line.

Teacher: You have used the facts you have learned about these animals to write an informative contrast paragraph. Your information is relevant and accurate.

The Comparison-Contrast Paragraph Framework

A *comparison-contrast paragraph* combines a comparison paragraph and a contrast paragraph. The framework consists of three sentences that offer comparisons, a transitional sentence, and three sentences that offer contrasts. The comparisons include the transitional words "both," "each," and "like." The contrasts include the transitional words "but," "yet," and "however." In general, students should compare or contrast physical characteristics first, then address less easily observed characteristics, such as habits and unusual traits

To develop a comparison-contrast paragraph, students must be able to:

- engage in discussions about an assigned topic and intellectually process information for relevance and accuracy

- categorize information (e.g., similarities and differences between two concrete nouns in the same category)

- think of subtle similarities and differences, which requires a deeper understanding of the concrete nouns they are examining

- use the transitional words "both," "each," and "like" to signal a comparison

- use the transitional words "but," "yet," and "however" to signal a contrast

- compose a transitional sentence that links the similarities and differences

The procedures below help students develop a topic sentence for the paragraph, provide specific points of comparison and contrast in the body of the paragraph, compose a transitional sentence, and develop a concluding sentence. These procedures are for use with the comparison-contrast framework. A sample framework follows.

FRAMEWORK FOR COMPARISON AND CONTRAST PARAGRAPH

Name: _____

Date: _____

Day: _____

Comparison and Contrast: ___*coyote*___ and ___*prairie fox*___

Question: ___*Do the coyote and the prairie fox share similarities and differences?*___

Topic sentence: ___*The coyote and the prairie fox share similarities and differences.*___
(Restate the question)

Similarities

both
each
like
also
same
similarly
have in common

grayish red fur
long, bushy tail
very shy

These animals share many likenesses, but they also have differences.

Transitional Sentence

Differences

but
yet
however
whereas
on the other hand
although

coyote		prairie fox
longer	legs	short
plain	muzzle	black smudge
pounces on jack rabbits	hunting style	zigzags after mice

Concluding Sentence: ___*The coyote and the prairie fox have some common characteristics and hunting habits; however,*___

___*their differences make it possible for them to share the same environment.*___

The Topic Sentence

The topic sentence compares and contrasts two concrete nouns in the same category. Students generate the statement from a cue question, which the teacher writes on the blackboard. Students copy the question from the board and then compose the topic sentence. For example:

Question: Do the coyote and the prairie fox share similarities and differences?

Topic sentence: The coyote and the prairie fox share similarities and differences.

The Body

The body of the paragraph includes comparison sentences and contrast sentences. First, students create three sentences that express similarities about the topic, using different transitional words to mark the comparisons. Next, students compose a transitional sentence that links the similarities to the differences. After that, students create three sentences that express differences about the topic, again using a variety of transitional words. Students create coherent paragraphs by focusing on accuracy, using synonyms to avoid repetition, and employing precise vocabulary.

The paragraphs below offer detailed instructions. They assume that the teacher has written the comparison-contrast paragraph framework on the blackboard, distributed the comparison-contrast framework as a worksheet, and helped students write the topic sentence.

The teacher holds up colored pictures of a coyote and a prairie fox and asks students to name the animals they see. The teacher writes "coyote" and "prairie fox" in the framework on the blackboard, beside the words "Comparison and Contrast." Students copy the words onto their frameworks.

In a turn-taking format, the teacher asks students to identify the characteristics these animals share. The teacher writes students' responses on the blackboard, under the heading "Similarities."

The teacher tells students that a transitional sentence acts as a segue from the similarities to the differences. The teacher asks a student for a transitional sentence and writes it on the blackboard, beside the words "Transitional Sentence."

Next, the teacher directs students' attention to the two boxes beneath the box labeled "Similarities." The teachers instructs students to write "coyote" on the first line in the box on the left and "prairie fox" on the first line in the box on the right.

The teacher asks the class for three points of contrast between the two animals and records them under the heading "Differences." The teacher lists physical differences first, followed by subtler differences. Students copy the three points onto their frameworks. The teacher then asks students, one at a time, to elaborate on the differences between the coyote and the prairie fox. The teacher writes the responses under the headings "coyote" and "prairie fox," as appropriate, and students copy them.

The teacher asks students to write the title "The Coyote and the Prairie Fox" on lined paper, skipping one line from the top. The teacher tells students to skip another line, indent, and copy the topic sentence. The teacher then directs students to use the framework to write the body of the comparison-contrast paragraph independently. The assignment is for students to:

- write three sentences describing how the coyote and prairie fox are similar, using different transitional words to mark each comparison

- copy the transitional sentence

- write three sentences describing how these animals are different, using a variety of transitional words to mark each contrast

The Concluding Sentence

The concluding sentence is an elaborated paraphrase of the topic sentence that incorporates the idea of similarity and contrast. To provide students with a reliable strategy, the teacher models elements of the sentence and asks students to paraphrase them and synthesize a conclusion.

> **Teacher**: You have explained how the coyote and the prairie fox are similar in some ways and different in other ways. Let's summarize how they are the same by saying they have common physical characteristics and hunting habits. Theresa, can you say that in your own words? Start your sentence with "the coyote and the prairie fox."

> **Theresa**: The coyote and the prairie fox have some common physical characteristics and hunting habits.

> **Teacher**: (Writes Theresa's response on the blackboard, ending it with a semicolon.) Nice job, Theresa. We also have to mention the

differences in the concluding sentence. The differences in these animals make it possible for them to share the same natural environment. State this idea in your own words. Start with the word "however." I'll read the first part of the concluding sentence: The coyote and the prairie fox have some common physical characteristics and hunting habits . . ."

Theresa: However, their differences make it possible for them to share the same environment.

Teacher: (Records Theresa's words on the blackboard.) Now read the whole concluding sentence.

Theresa: The coyote and the prairie fox have some common physical characteristics and hunting habits; however, their differences make it possible for them to share the same environment.

Teacher: The concluding sentence connects the ideas in the paragraph and lets the reader know that the paragraph has compared and contrasted information.

Putting It Together

The teacher writes the comparison-contrast framework and topic sentence question on the blackboard, then distributes comparison-contrast paragraph frameworks as worksheets. Students copy the topic sentence question from the board and independently restate it as a topic sentence. The teacher holds up colored pictures of a coyote and a prairie fox.

Teacher: Sam, what animals are we comparing and contrasting? I'll write your answer on the board.

Sam: A coyote and a prairie fox.

Teacher: Yes, we're comparing and contrasting a coyote and a prairie fox. You have already written a paragraph comparing these animals, as well as a paragraph that describes their differences. You know how to use the transitional words to signal comparisons and contrasts. Today, you will write a comparison-contrast paragraph independently, once we've shared the ideas and you've copied them onto your worksheets. Let's start with the similarities. Think about the physical characteristics as well as those not so easily observed. I'll write your responses on the board. Bill, how are these animals similar?

Bill: They have grayish-red fur.

Teacher: Good, Bill. (Writes his response on the blackboard.) Theresa, how else are they the same?

Theresa: They both have a long, bushy tail.

Teacher: Yes, they do. (Writes her response on the blackboard.) Sam, can you think of a less observable characteristic that these animals share?

Sam: These are very shy animals.

Teacher: (Writes his response on the blackboard.) You know a lot about the coyote and the prairie fox. Next, you are going to think about how they are different from each other. But before you do that, you need a sentence that links the two ideas. You need to prepare the reader for the shift from similarities to differences. This is called a transitional sentence. It is a paraphrase of the topic sentence. Bill, can you restate the topic sentence in your own words? Think of synonyms for "coyote," "prairie fox," and "similarities." Use the word "but" when you talk about differences.

Bill: These animals share many likenesses, but they also have differences.

Teacher: Excellent work, Bill. Read the transitional sentence back, and I'll write it on the board. Then you copy it. (Waits until the class finishes copying.) Let's look at the two boxes beneath the "Similarities" box. Write "coyote" in the left box and "prairie fox" in the right box. Use the line at the top of each box. (Writes the words on the blackboard.) Now you need to think of three ideas that show contrast. (As students respond, writes "size," "muzzle," and "hunting" under the heading "Differences.") Sam, how do the coyote and the prairie fox differ in size?

Sam: The coyote has longer legs and is taller. The prairie fox is a small, short animal.

Teacher: (Writes Sam's response under "coyote" and "prairie fox." Leads the class through the same process for the next two contrast ideas.) Theresa, how are the muzzles of these animals different?

Theresa: The coyote has a plain muzzle, and the prairie fox has a black smudge on his muzzle.

Teacher: Bill, how do the coyote and the prairie fox hunt their prey?

Bill: The coyote pounces on jackrabbits. The prairie fox zigzags as he chases mice.

Teacher: (Hands out lined paper and directs students to skip a line.) What is the title of this paragraph?

Class: The Coyote and the Prairie Fox.

Teacher: I'll write the title on the left side of the board. You copy it in the center of your paper. What's next, Sam?

Sam: We skip a line and indent and copy the topic sentence.

Teacher: That's right. Today you will work independently and write about how the coyote and prairie fox are both the same and different. Use the strategies you learned for writing comparison and contrast sentences. Once you finish the similarities for the coyote and the prairie fox, copy the transitional sentence. Then compose sentences that explain their differences. We'll think of a concluding sentence together.

The teacher then models the concluding sentence by stating the general characteristics that the students are comparing and contrasting.

Teacher: You have explained how the coyote and the prairie fox are similar in some ways and different in other ways. Let's summarize how they are the same by saying they have common physical characteristics and hunting habits. Theresa, can you say that in your own words? Start your sentence with "the coyote and the prairie fox."

Theresa: The coyote and the prairie fox have some common physical characteristics and hunting habits.

Teacher: (Writes Theresa's response on the blackboard, followed by a semicolon.) Nice job, Theresa. We also have to mention the differences in the concluding sentence. The differences in these animals make it possible for them to share the same natural environment. State this idea in your own words. Start with the word "however." I'll read the first part of the concluding sentence: The coyote and the prairie fox have some common physical characteristics and hunting habits: . . .

Theresa: However, their differences make it possible for them to share the same environment.

Teacher: (Writes Theresa's words on the blackboard.) Now read the whole concluding sentence, Theresa.

Theresa: The coyote and the prairie fox have some common physical characteristics and hunting habits; however, their differences make it possible for them to share the same environment

Teacher: The concluding sentence connects the ideas in the paragraph and lets the reader know that the paragraph has compared and contrasted information.

A sample of the finished comparison-contrast paragraph follows.

Student's Paragraph Copied from Comparison-Contrast Framework

The Coyote and the Prairie Fox

The coyote and the prairie fox share many similarities and differences. Both the coyote and the prairie fox have grayish red fur. Each of them possesses a long, bushy tail. In addition, they are very shy. These animals share many likenesses, but they also have differences. The coyote has longer legs and is taller, whereas the prairie fox is a small, short animal. The prairie fox displays a black smudge on his muzzle; on the other hand, the coyote has a plain muzzle. The coyote pounces on jack rabbits, yet the prairie fox zigzags as he chases mice. The coyote and the prairie fox have some common physical characteristics and hunting habits; however, their differences make it possible for them to share the same environment.

The Brief Essay Framework

Students who can write different types of expository paragraphs on concrete topics are ready to write a brief essay. The *brief essay* focuses on less concrete topics and requires students to think about what they can less easily observe. The framework for a brief essay is three sentences that support the topic, marked by the transitional expressions "first of all," "secondly," and "thirdly." An elaborating sentence that gives more information follows each supporting sentence. All sentences are arranged in a clear, logical order.

To write three sentences that support the topic, plus an elaborating sentence for each, students must be able to:

- engage in discussions about an assigned topic and intellectually process information for relevance and accuracy

- categorize information (e.g., break an assigned topic down into smaller components)

- provide clear examples that support the topic sentence

- make inferences that respond to *why* and *how* questions

The procedures below help students develop a topic sentence for a brief essay, write supporting sentences and elaborating sentences in the body of the paragraph, and compose a concluding sentence. These procedures are for use with the essay framework. A sample essay framework follows on the next page.

The Topic Sentence

A brief essay begins with a topic sentence that needs the support of clear, logical ideas. Teachers can cue students for the topic sentence with a question. For example:

Question: Did the pioneers face many problems as they traveled west?

Topic sentence: The pioneers faced many problems as they traveled west.

The Body

The body of a brief essay supports the topic sentence. The transitional expressions "first of all," "secondly," and "thirdly" mark each sentence that

FRAMEWORK FOR BRIEF ESSAY

> Capitalization
> Handwriting
> Omission of Words
> Punctuation
> Spelling

Name: _____

Date: _____

Day: _____

Question: *Did the pioneers face many problems as they traveled west?*

_____

Topic Sentence:

(Restate the question) *The pioneers faced many problems as they traveled west.*

_____

First of all, *First of all, they sometimes were caught in spring blizzards.*

Why?/How? *The temperature dropped below freezing on the plains and the pioneers and animals froze to death.*

Secondly, *Secondly, some of the wagons overturned in the rivers if they were flooded.*

Why?/How? *The current was too strong for the pioneers to control the wagons as they drifted across.*

Thirdly, *Thirdly, many children and old people caught bad colds and died from pneumonia.*

Why?/How? *There usually weren't any doctors on the wagon trains, and the pioneers only had simple medicines to help the sick.*

Concluding Sentence: *In conclusion, the pioneers faced serious problems such as weather, accidents and sickness, and it took a lot of courage to overcome them.*

supports the topic sentence. Each of these sentences is followed by another sentence, which gives more information. The inference answers the question *why* or, occasionally, *how*. Students create a coherent essay by focusing on accurate information, logical inferences, and precise vocabulary. They write in the present tense unless the topic is of historical interest.

The paragraphs below offer detailed instructions. They assume that the teacher has written the essay framework on the blackboard, distributed the essay framework as a worksheet, and helped students write the topic sentence.

The teacher asks students what problems the pioneers faced as they traveled west across the plains. One at a time, students brainstorm the problems while the teacher writes them on the left side of the blackboard. Students choose the three problems they want to write about from the finished list, and the teacher circles them. Before they start composing sentences, the teacher asks whether students are satisfied with the sequence of the problems and makes any adjustments.

One at a time, students compose supporting sentences that begin with the transitional expressions "first of all," "secondly," and "thirdly." The teacher writes the sentences into the framework on the blackboard. Students read the sentences back and make any necessary changes before copying them onto their frameworks.

The teacher reads each supporting sentence and restates it as a question. The teacher begins the question with "why" or, occasionally, "how." For example:

> **Sentence**: First of all, the wagon train sometimes was caught in spring blizzards.
>
> **Why question**: Why was the wagon train sometimes caught in spring blizzards?
>
> **How question**: How did it make a difference if the wagon train was caught in spring blizzards?

Once students can respond to a why question, the teacher teaches them to generate one by restating a sentence. Students develop more logical responses with this procedure. The teacher then introduces how questions in the same manner: by modeling how questions for students to answer, then asking students to generate their own how questions by restating sentences.

If-then sentences are excellent responses to the question *how*. For example:

> **Supporting sentence**: First of all, the wagon train sometimes was caught in spring blizzards.
>
> **Teacher**: How did it make a difference if the wagon train was caught in spring blizzards?
>
> **Student**: If the temperature suddenly dropped below freezing on the plains, then the pioneers and animals froze to death.

The Concluding Sentence

The concluding sentence directly relates to the topic sentence. Students often need guiding questions to synthesize information for a concluding sentence. The teacher models the pattern below and asks students to paraphrase the information in a concluding sentence.

> **Teacher**: Did the pioneers face serious problems traveling west, such as weather, accidents, and sickness? Did it take a lot of courage to overcome them? Who can paraphrase this information in a concluding sentence?
>
> **Student**: The pioneers faced serious problems traveling west, such as weather, accidents, and sickness, and it took a lot of courage to overcome them.

Putting It Together

The teacher writes the brief essay framework and topic sentence question on the blackboard, then hands out frameworks. Students copy the topic sentence question from the board and independently restate it as a topic sentence.

> **Teacher**: We have been talking about the problems the pioneers faced as they traveled west. Let's start with you, Theresa, and brainstorm some of them. I'll write them on the blackboard for you.
>
> **Theresa**: Let's see . . . weather. The pioneers didn't always have good weather.
>
> **Teacher**: (Writes "weather" on the blackboard.) Give me some examples, Theresa.

Theresa: Well, sometimes there was a late spring blizzard. They had droughts, too, and there wasn't enough water.

Teacher: You have learned a lot. Bill, think of another problem the pioneers faced.

Bill: People drowned, wagons overturned.

Teacher: What category is that, Bill? Did the pioneers want these things to happen?

Bill: No, they didn't. Those were accidents.

Teacher: Good. (Writes "accidents" on the blackboard.) You were giving me specific examples of problems rather than ideas about the problems the pioneers faced. Sam, give me another example of a problem the pioneers faced.

Sam: The pioneers got wet and they often came down with bad colds that turned into pneumonia. (Pause.) They got very sick.

Teacher: (Writes "sickness" on the blackboard.) Yes, they had to face serious illness. They didn't have doctors and used simple home remedies for medicine. I have a problem to share with you. The pioneers sometimes lost their way when they tried to take a shortcut. (Writes "getting lost" on the blackboard.) OK, what three ideas do you want to write about to support the topic sentence? (Students choose "weather," "accidents," and "sickness.") Do you like the order in which we are going to write about them? (Numbers the list in order.)

The teacher asks students to write the word "weather" above the transitional expression "first of all," the word "accidents" above "secondly," and the word "sickness" above "thirdly." This memory aid helps students organize their sentences.

Teacher: Theresa, it's your turn to compose the first sentence, about weather. Remember to start the sentence with "first of all." I'll write the sentence on the blackboard, you read it back, and the class will copy it.

Theresa: First of all, the pioneers . . . the wagon train sometimes got . . . was caught in blizzards.

Teacher: That's true, but what time of the year was it when this happened? The wagon trains left Independence, Missouri, as early in the spring as possible.

Theresa: Spring blizzards. First of all, the wagon train sometimes was caught in spring blizzards.

Teacher: Right. (Writes Theresa's sentence on the blackboard. The class copies it.) Bill?

Bill: Secondly, some of the wagons overturned in the rivers if they were flooded.

Teacher: Good. (Writes Bill's sentence on the blackboard. The class copies it.) Sam?

Sam: Thirdly, many children died from bad colds.

Teacher: You're right, but was it just the children who died?

Sam: Old people died, too.

Teacher: What happens when you don't take care of a bad cold? (Long pause.) You get pneu-.

Sam: Pneumonia.

Teacher: Good. Now restate your sentence.

Sam: Thirdly, many children and old people got . . . caught bad colds and died from pneumonia.

Teacher: (Writes Sam's sentence on the blackboard. The class copies it.) You've done a fine job supporting the topic sentence with specific information. Now we need to explain why something happened or how it made a difference. Read the sentences, starting with the first one, then respond to the why or how question I ask.

Bill: First of all, the wagon train sometimes was caught in spring blizzards.

Teacher: How did it make a difference if the wagon train sometimes was caught in spring blizzards? Remember to begin your answer with "if."

Bill: If the temperature suddenly dropped below freezing on the plains, then the pioneers and animals froze to death.

Teacher: Good. Theresa?

Theresa: Secondly, some of the wagons overturned in the rivers if they were flooded.

Teacher: Why did the wagons overturn if the rivers were flooded? Was there a strong current?

Theresa: The current was too strong for the pioneers to control the wagons.

Teacher: Excellent. Sam?

Sam: Thirdly, many children and old people caught bad colds and died from pneumonia.

Teacher: Why did many children and old people catch bad colds and die from pneumonia? Did they have doctors on the wagon trains? What about medicine?

Sam: There usually weren't any doctors on the wagon trains, and the pioneers only had simple medicines to help the sick.

Teacher: You have done a great job thinking of specific responses to elaborate on your sentences. I like the way you take the time to organize what you want to say. You also are making good use of your background knowledge about pioneer life on the plains. Let's think of a strong concluding sentence for this essay.

The teacher provides modeling to help students develop a concluding sentence that ties in all the information and relates to the topic sentence.

Teacher: Let's think of a strong concluding sentence for this essay. Did the pioneers face serious problems traveling west, such as weather, accidents, and sickness? Did it take a lot of courage to overcome them? Who can paraphrase this information in a concluding sentence?

Sam: The pioneers faced serious problems traveling west, such as weather, accidents, and sickness, and it took a lot of courage to overcome them.

A sample of the finished essay follows on the next page.

Elaborating on a Brief Essay

Once students can write a brief essay with occasional teacher guidance, they are ready to elaborate on why and how inferences with facts.

Teacher: You can now supply logical ideas for the supporting sentences in your brief essays. Next you are going to write an essay that elaborates on these ideas by following your why and how responses with a fact. You already learned to use facts in enumerative, comparison, and contrast paragraphs. Sam, you read the first idea and supply the additional information.

Student's Paragraph Copied from the Brief Essay Framework

The Problems of Pioneers Traveling West

The pioneers faced many problems as they traveled west. First of all, they sometimes were caught in spring blizzards. The temperature dropped below freezing on the plains and the pioneers and animals froze to death. Secondly, some of the wagons overturned in the rivers if they were flooded. The current was too strong for the pioneers to control the wagons as they drifted across. Thirdly, many children and old people caught bad colds and died from pneumonia. There usually weren't any doctors on the wagon trains, and the pioneers only had simple medicines to help the sick. In conclusion, the pioneers faced serious problems such as weather, accidents and sickness, and it took a lot of courage to overcome them.

Sam: First of all, the wagon train sometimes was caught in spring blizzards. Why? The pioneers took a chance and left Missouri as early in the spring as possible. How? If the temperature suddenly dropped below freezing on the plains, then the pioneers and animals froze to death. Fact: Strong winds blew the snow into deep drifts that covered the wagons.

Students elaborate on the second and third supporting sentences in the same way.

Transitioning from a Single- to a Multiple-Paragraph Structure

Once students can write an elaborated brief essay, the teacher can demonstrate how to create three paragraphs by repeating the framework for a single paragraph. Exercise 8 outlines a three-paragraph structure. Each paragraph has four or five sentences.

Although two-sentence paragraphs can be viable, teachers should encourage weaker students to work beyond that minimum standard. One option is for students to create a three-paragraph essay that does not incorporate a fact sentence or that omits one of the inferential sentences. However, students with less flexible language abilities benefit greatly from learning to infer information, which a well-developed essay requires.

Exercise 8
A Multiple-Paragraph Structure

First Paragraph

1. Topic sentence

2. Supporting sentence ("first of all")

3. Why inferential sentence

4. How inferential sentence

5. Specific fact

Second Paragraph

1. Supporting sentence ("secondly")

2. Why inferential sentence

3. How inferential sentence

4. Specific fact

Third Paragraph

1. Supporting sentence ("thirdly")

2. Why inferential sentence

3. How inferential sentence

4. Specific fact

5. Concluding sentence

Sentence Frameworks

Landmark School, Inc.

KERNEL SENTENCE FRAMEWORK

Name: _____

Date: _____

Day: _____

WORD BOX for INANIMATE NOUNS
sat lay stood rested leaned
hovered stretched hung spread

Article	Noun	Action Verb-ed

From *Talking to Writing*, Jennings + Haynes, 2002

EXPANDED KERNEL SENTENCE FRAMEWORK

Name: _____

Date: _____

Day: _____

WORD BOX for INANIMATE NOUNS
sat   lay   stood   rested   leaned
hovered   stretched   hung   spread

Article	Noun	Action Verb-ed	Where Phrase

Expanded Kernel Sentence Framework

Name: _____

Date: _____

Day: _____

WHEN PHRASES
parts of the day
weather
units of time

WORD BOX for INANIMATE NOUNS
sat   lay   stood   rested   leaned
hovered   stretched   hung   spread

Article	Noun	Action Verb-ed	Where Phrase	When Phrase

From *Talking to Writing.* Jennings + Haynes, 2002

Expanded Kernel Sentence Framework

Name: _____

Date: _____

Day: _____

Easy 4

1. _____

2. _____

3. _____

4. _____

| WORD BOX for INANIMATE NOUNS |
| sat   lay   stood   rested   leaned |
| hovered   stretched   hung   spread |

Article	Adjective	Noun	Action Verb-ed

Expanded Kernel Sentence Framework

Easy 4

1. _____
2. _____
3. _____
4. _____

Name: _____
Date: _____
Day: _____

WORD BOX for INANIMATE NOUNS
sat   lay   stood   rested   leaned
hovered   stretched   hung   spread

Article	Adjective	Noun	Action Verb-ed	Where Phrase

From *Talking to Writing*, Jennings + Haynes, 2002

Expanded Kernel Sentence Framework

Easy 4

1. _____
2. _____
3. _____
4. _____

Name: _____
Date: _____
Day: _____

WORD BOX for INANIMATE NOUNS
sat   lay   stood   rested   leaned
hovered   stretched   hung   spread

WHEN PHRASES
parts of the day
weather
units of time

Article	Adjective	Noun	Action Verb-ed	When Phrase

Expanded Kernel Sentence Framework

Easy 4	6 Senses	Hard 3
1. _____	5. _____	1. _____
2. _____	6. _____	2. _____
3. _____	7. _____	3. _____
4. _____	8. _____	
	9. _____	

Name: _____
Date: _____
Day: _____

WORD BOX for INANIMATE NOUNS
sat lay stood rested leaned
hovered stretched hung spread

WHEN PHRASES
parts of the day
weather
units of time

Article	Adjective	Adjective	Noun	Action Verb-ed	Where Phrase	When Phrase

Landmark School, Inc.

From *Talking to Writing*, Jennings + Haynes, 2002

Expanded Kernel Sentence Framework
Adverb (ly)

Name: _____
Date: _____
Day: _____

WORD BOX for INANIMATE NOUNS
sat lay stood rested leaned
hovered stretched hung spread

Article	Noun	Action Verb-ed	Adverb (ly)

EXPANDED KERNEL SENTENCE FRAMEWORK
Temporal Clause

Name: _____

Date: _____

Day: _____

WORD BOX for WHEN WORDS

as   as soon as   when   whenever
while   until   once   after   before
since

WORD BOX for INANIMATE NOUNS

sat   lay   stood   rested   leaned
hovered   stretched   hung   spread

Article	Noun	Action Verb-ed	Where Phrase	when word	noun	verb-ed

Landmark School, Inc.

From *Talking to Writing*, Jennings + Haynes, 2002

EXPANDED KERNEL SENTENCE FRAMEWORK
Object Dependent Clause

Name: _____
Date: _____
Day: _____

Article	Noun	Action Verb-ed	who/which/ that	verb-ed

Landmark School, Inc.

EXPANDED KERNEL SENTENCE FRAMEWORK
Subject Dependent Clause

Name: _____
Date: _____
Day: _____

Article	Noun,	who/which/ that	verb-ed,	Action Verb-ed

From *Talking to Writing*, Jennings + Haynes, 2002

Paragraph and Essay Frameworks

FRAMEWORK FOR OBJECT DESCRIPTION

Name: _____

Date: _____

Day: _____

Description of: _____

Topic Sentence:

Topic Noun + is/are + Category + who/which/that + General Appearance

_____ / _____ / _____ / _____ / _____

Key Features:

Article	Adjective	Adjective	Noun	Function Verb

Concluding Sentence: _____

Landmark School, Inc.

From *Talking to Writing*, Jennings + Haynes, 2002

FRAMEWORK FOR PROCESS PARAGRAPH

Name: _____

Date: _____

Day: _____

Question: _____

Topic Sentence:

(Restate the question) _____

_____

First, _____

_____

Why?/How? _____

_____

Then, _____

Why?/How? _____

_____

Next, _____

Why?/How? _____

_____

After that, _____

Why?/How? _____

_____

Finally, _____

_____

Why?/How? _____

_____

Concluding Sentence: _____

_____

From *Talking to Writing*, Jennings + Haynes, 2002

Landmark School, Inc.

FRAMEWORK FOR ENUMERATIVE PARAGRAPH

Name: _____

Date: _____

Day: _____

Question: _____

_____

Topic Sentence:

(Restate the question) _____

_____

First of all, _____

_____

Fact: _____

_____

Secondly, _____

_____

Fact: _____

_____

Thirdly, _____

_____

Fact: _____

_____

Concluding Sentence: _____

_____

From *Talking to Writing*, Jennings + Haynes, 2002

FRAMEWORK FOR COMPARISON PARAGRAPH

Name: _____

Date: _____

Day: _____

Comparison of: _____ and _____

Synonyms	Similarities
_____	1. _____
_____	2. _____
_____	3. _____

Question: _____

Topic Sentence: _____

    (Restate the question)

1. _____

    _____

2. _____

    _____

3. _____

    _____

Concluding Sentence: _____

    _____

both   **each**   **like**

Landmark School, Inc.

FRAMEWORK FOR CONTRAST PARAGRAPH

Name: _____

Date: _____

Day: _____

Contrast of: _____ and _____

Characteristics

Differences		Differences
1. _____	⟷	1. _____
2. _____	⟷	2. _____
3. _____	⟷	3. _____

Question: _____

Topic Sentence: _____
                    (Restate the question)

1. _____

_____

2. _____

_____

3. _____

_____

Concluding Sentence: _____

_____

but   yet   however

From *Talking to Writing*. Jennings + Haynes, 2002

FRAMEWORK FOR COMPARISON AND CONTRAST PARAGRAPH

Name: _____

Date: _____

Day: _____

Comparison and Contrast: _____ and _____

Question: _____

Topic sentence: _____

(Restate the question)

Similarities

_____
_____
_____
_____

both
each
like
also
same
similarly
have in common

Transitional Sentence

Differences

_____
_____
_____
_____

_____
_____
_____
_____

but
yet
however
whereas
on the other hand
although

Concluding Sentence: _____

FRAMEWORK FOR BRIEF ESSAY

| **C**apitalization |
| **H**andwriting |
| **O**mission of Words |
| **P**unctuation |
| **S**pelling |

Name: _____

Date: _____

Day: _____

Question: _____

_____

Topic Sentence:

(Restate the question) _____

_____

First of all, _____

_____

Why?/How? _____

_____

Secondly, _____

_____

Why?/How? _____

_____

Thirdly, _____

_____

Why?/How? _____

_____

Concluding Sentence: _____

_____

From *Talking to Writing*, Jennings + Haynes, 2002

Oral Expression Skills

The Landmark curriculum for oral expression has two goals: to improve students' ability to share information and to engage them in goal-oriented social communication. The auditory curriculum is based on the principle that verbal language must be correctly processed and understood for accurate, meaningful oral production to follow. When assessed under sufficiently demanding conditions, dyslexic students exhibit deficits in one or more of these linguistic areas: phonology (speech sounds), morphology (meaningful word parts), syntax (sentence structure), semantics (vocabulary, meaning), and pragmatics (multisentence level of discourse, social communication skills). To promote improved phonological skills, students are trained to discriminate speech sounds, associate speech sounds with letter symbols, and identify syllable units within words. Through direct instruction in each of these areas, students are immersed in the rules and structure of the English language.

Phonology

- Articulate speech sounds efficiently
- Rhyme words
- Discriminate initial consonant sounds
- Discriminate final consonant sounds
- Discriminate medial consonant sounds
- Discriminate short vowel sounds
- Discriminate long vowel sounds
- Discriminate initial consonant blends
- Discriminate final consonant blends
- Discriminate diphthongs
- Discriminate consonant digraphs
- Recognize and produce correct number of syllables in multisyllabic words
- Recognize and produce correct number of syllables in sentences

Landmark School, Inc.

- Recognize and produce correct sequence of syllables in multi-syllabic words
- Take dictation of consonant-vowel-consonant (cvc) words
- Take dictation of consonant-vowel-consonant words with blends
- Take dictation of consonant-vowel-consonant words with digraphs
- Take dictation of words following the cvc/cvc pattern (e.g., cat-nip)
- Take dictation of words following the cvc/cvc pattern with blends
- Take dictation of words following the cvc/cvc pattern with digraphs
- Take dictation of words following the cvc/cvc pattern with blends and digraphs
- Take dictation of multisyllabic words with blends and digraphs
- Take dictation of words with open and closed syllables
- Take dictation of multisyllabic words
- Write sentences containing five to eight words
- Retain and follow three to four oral directions
- Retain and follow three to four oral directions in sequence
- Retain and recite poems

Morphology

- Recognize and produce past tense of regular verbs
- Recognize and produce past tense of selected irregular verbs
- Recognize and produce past participle of regular verbs
- Recognize and produce past participle of selected irregular verbs
- Recognize and produce selected prefixes
- Recognize and produce selected suffixes

- Recognize and produce regular plurals
- Recognize and produce irregular plurals

Semantics

- Recognize and produce full names of classmates
- Recognize and name elements belonging to a specific category
- Recognize and name category labels for selected lists of elements
- Recognize and name elements a specific category
- Recognize and name synonyms to expand vocabulary
- Recognize and name antonyms to expand vocabulary
- Recognize and name multiple-meaning words
- Recognize and name adjectival descriptions of objects
- Recognize and name category labels for low-level adjective groups
- Recognize and name category labels for mid-level adjective groups
- Recognize and produce description of various objects' functions
- Recognize and name spatial concepts
- Recognize and name cautionary and informative terms
- Recognize and produce figurative language

Syntax

- Recognize and produce pronouns and articles
- Recognize and produce article-noun agreement
- Recognize and produce subject-verb agreement
- Recognize and produce nouns vs. verbs
- Recognize and produce complete simple sentences

- Recognize and produce prepositional phrases indicating place
- Recognize and produce prepositional phrases indicating time
- Recognize and produce simple sentences with prepositional phrases *where* and *when*
- Recognize and produce adjectives vs. other parts of speech
- Recognize and produce adjectives in simple sentences
- Recognize and produce adjectives in simple sentences with phrases *where* and *when*
- Recognize and produce adverbs vs. other parts of speech
- Recognize and produce adverbs in simple sentences
- Recognize and produce adverbs in simple sentences with phrases *where* and *when*
- Recognize and produce compound sentences linked by "and" or "but"
- Recognize and produce complex sentences "because"
- Recognize and produce complex sentences containing adverbial clauses
- Recognize and produce complex sentences containing object-dependent relative clauses
- Recognize and produce complex sentences containing subject-dependent relative clauses
- Recognize and produce interrogative sentences

Listening Comprehension

- Understand directions
- Discern main idea of orally presented material
- Recall details
- Remember sequence of ideas and events
- Draw conclusions
- Summarize paragraphs/stories orally
- Develop outlines from orally presented material
- Take notes on orally presented material
- Develop test-taking techniques

Oral Expression

- Give accurate/concise oral directions
- Describe objects/pictures using feature and subordinate details
- Describe an event or process using transitional words
- Organize and describe comparisons and contrasts
- Express and support an opinion
- Give concise oral summaries
- Deliver structured narrative (setting, plot, resolution)
- Open and close a telephone conversation
- Include relevant information in phone conversations
- Deliver organized prepared speeches

Pragmatics/Discourse

- Ask socially appropriate, topically relevant questions
- Use appropriate language in context
- Use turn-taking at appropriate times in conversation
- Decrease interruptive behavior
- Recognize other individuals' perspective (logical)
- Recognize other individuals' perspective (emotion)
- Give and accept constructive criticism
- Use appropriate eye contact (speaking and listening)
- Monitor vocal loudness
- Monitor vocal intonation (loudness, rate, pitch)
- Monitor and employ clear enunciation
- Monitor and employ appropriate gestures
- Monitor and employ appropriate fluency
- Monitor and employ appropriate posture
- Monitor and employ appropriate grooming (hygiene, dress)

Written Expression Skills

Assessments of Landmark students' written expression levels generally show a need for increased skills and considerable growth before students can succeed at grade-level expectations. The priority in language arts class at Landmark is to address students' need to access language and express themselves in writing. Emphasis is on developing oral-to-written expression (talking, listening, discussing, analyzing, and brainstorming ideas before writing). Thematic units, such as the Wild West and ancient Egypt, provide the basis for all instruction, along with a structured linguistic approach to teaching language skills. Teachers use theme-related pictures to tap into students' visual abilities, stimulate word retrieval, and foster contextual associations.

Language arts class requires extensive practice generating complete sentences (expanded kernel, compound, and complex sentences), single paragraphs, and multiple paragraphs. Lessons in capitalization and punctuation are presented within the context of written expression. Teachers emphasize awareness of the sounds and syllable structure of words, and students are encouraged to use phonetic spelling to represent new or unfamiliar words. Efficient handwriting is stressed. Emphasis is on identifying and generating specific nouns, action verbs, prepositional phrases, and adjectives; accurate use of these words in context is a focus as well. Adverbs are taught once students master adjectival description.

Identifying the Alphabet

- Sequence the alphabet (oral)
- Sequence the alphabet (written)

Organizing and Copying

- Organize work effectively on paper
- Use lower-case cursive letter formations
- Use upper-case cursive letter formations
- Copy accurately from a near point
- Copy accurately from a far point

- Provide friendly letter heading
- Provide friendly letter greeting
- Provide friendly letter closing
- Employ phonetic spelling

Semantics

- Recognize and provide elements belonging to a specific category
- Recognize and provide relevant vs. irrelevant information in a list
- Recognize and provide category labels for a given list of elements
- Provide synonyms
- Provide antonyms
- Provide adjectival description
- Provide category labels for low-level adjective groups
- Provide category labels for mid-level adjective groups
- Provide adverbial description
- Provide category labels for introductory adverb groups
- Provide category labels for mid-adverb groups
- Recognize and produce similes
- Recognize and produce metaphors

Syntax

- Provide article-plus-noun agreement
- Provide specific nouns
- Provide inanimate nouns
- Provide simple past-tense verbs
- Associate simple past-tense verbs with inanimate nouns
- Provide complete simple sentences
- Provide noun-plus-verb agreement

- Provide prepositional phrases place
- Provide prepositional phrases time
- Expand simple sentences with prepositional phrases
- Provide adjectives in kernel sentences
- Provide adjectives in simple sentences with prepositional phrases *where* and *when*
- Provide accurate use of vocabulary in context
- Provide declarative sentences
- Provide interrogative sentences
- Provide imperative sentences
- Provide exclamatory sentences
- Provide compound sentences linked by "and"
- Provide compound sentences linked by "but"
- Provide complex sentences linked by "because"
- Provide prepositional phrases that introduce simple sentences
- Provide sentences with quotations
- Provide adverbs in kernel sentences
- Provide adverbs in simple sentences containing *where* prepositional phrases
- Provide complex sentences with temporal adverbial clauses
- Provide complex sentences with spatial adverbial clauses
- Provide complex sentences with object-dependent relative clauses
- Provide complex sentences with subject-dependent relative clauses

Mechanics

- Capitalize the beginning of sentences
- Capitalize proper nouns
- Produce abbreviations

- Capitalize abbreviations
- Produce punctuation (period, question mark, exclamation point)
- Observe comma rules
- Use quotations

Paragraph Writing

Provide the friendly letter

Provide the basic paragraph

Select a topic within an assigned theme

Provide a lead or topic sentence

Sequence information logically

Provide sufficient detail to support the topic

Provide relevant detail to support the topic

Follow a framework to write a paragraph

Eliminate sentence fragments

Eliminate run-on sentences

Use consistent verb tense

Provide a variety of sentence structures

Provide transitional words (first, then, next, after that, finally)

Provide transitional phrases

Provide a conclusion

Produce a sequenced personal narrative paragraph

Produce a descriptive paragraph

Produce a process paragraph

Produce an enumerative paragraph

Produce a sequenced theme-related narrative paragraph

Produce a comparison paragraph

Produce a contrast paragraph

Produce a comparison-contrast paragraph

Produce a brief essay

Produce a short report

Use the computer to write a final draft

Multi-Paragraph Writing

- Produce setting and plot/problem paragraph for a narrative
- Produce setting plot/problem and resolution paragraph for a narrative
- Produce an essay
- Produce a thesis paragraph
- Generate relevant details
- Explain inferences
- Provide additional information
- Provide transitional sentences
- Provide a concluding paragraph

Study Skills

- Select information from brief passages
- Fill in a paragraph framework independently
- Paraphrase concisely
- Summarize from written sources
- Summarize from oral sources
- Alphabetize words
- Identify the function and location of guide words
- Use guide words to locate entries
- Locate primary definitions

Research and Library Skills

- Choose and limit a topic
- Gather information

- Use card catalog
- Use encyclopedia
- Use periodicals
- Use the computer to research a topic

Proofreading

- Edit written work for specific sentence skills
- Edit paragraphs for specific composition skills
- Use the computer for editing

Transitional Words and Phrases

Purpose	*Words and Phrases*
To sequence events	First, then, next, after that, finally
To list a series of ideas	First of all, secondly, thirdly
To compare ideas	Both, each, like, also, same, similarly, have in common
To contrast ideas	But, yet, however, whereas, on the other hand, although
To summarize or conclude	In conclusion, to conclude, to sum up, all in all, overall

Landmark School, Inc.

References

Adams, M. 1990. *Beginning to read: Thinking and learning about print. A summary.* Cambridge: MIT Press.

Bell, N. 1991. *Visualizing and verbalizing for language comprehension and thinking.* rev. ed. Paso Robles, CA: Academy of Reading Publications.

Berninger, V. 1999. The "write stuff" for preventing and treating writing disabilities. *Perspectives, International Dyslexia Association* 25 (2):20–22 (spring).

Caswell, L., and N. Duke. 1998. Non-narrative as a catalyst for writing development. *Language Arts* 75:108–17.

Cohen, E., R. Sevcik, and M. Wolf. 1999. The RAVE-O curriculum. *Perspectives, International Dyslexia Association* 25 (2):17–19 (spring).

Fawcett, S., and A. Sandberg. 1988. *Evergreen: A guide to writing.* Boston: Houghton Mifflin.

Haynes, C., and T. Jennings. 1992. *Thematic instruction: A teacher's primer for developing speaking and writing skills.* Prides Crossing, MA: Landmark Foundation.

Lindamood, P. 1998. *LiPS: Lindamood phoneme sequencing. Austin: Pro-Ed.*

Lyon, R. 1997. Learning to read: A call from research to action. Statement before the Committee on Education and the Workforce, 10 July, at the U.S. House of Representatives, Washington, D.C.

Nagy, W. 1988. *Teaching vocabulary to aid reading comprehension.* Newark, DE: International Reading Association.

Norris, J., and P. Hoffman. 1993. *Whole language intervention for the classroom.* San Diego: Singular Publishing Group.

Paul, R. 2000. *Language disorders from infancy through adolescence: Assessment and intervention*, Second Edition. Boston: Mosby.

Robertson, C., and W. Salter. 1995. *The phonological awareness kit (primary and secondary).* E. Moline, IL: Linguisystems.

Singer, B., and A. Bashir. "What Are Executive Functions and Self-Regulation and What Do They Have to Do with Language Learning Disorders?" *Language, Speech, and Hearing Services in the Schools* 3, no. 3 (1999):265–73.

Westby, C. 1991. *Steps to developing and achieving a language-based curriculum in the classroom.* Rockville, MD: ASHA.

Wiig, E., and E. Semel. 1984. *Language assessment and intervention for the learning disabled.* Ohio: Merrill.

Glossary

attend. To focus selectively on an object or idea in the presence of distracters, including but not limited to auditory or visual stimuli.

attention. The act of attending.

brainstorming. A teaching strategy for activating students' knowledge of vocabulary and theme-related concepts. Incorporates three overlapping and sequential phases: stimulation, guidance, and recording.

complex sentence. A sentence that contains at least one independent and dependent clause. For example, "When lightning struck, the cattle stampeded." Although the clause "When lightning struck" has a subject (lightning) and a verb (struck), the clause is dependent because it cannot stand by itself. A dependent clause is also called an embedded clause because it is affixed to or inserted into a standalone sentence (the independent clause). The clause "the cattle stampeded" is independent because it can stand by itself.

compound sentence. A sentence that combines two or more independent clauses. For example, "Lightning struck and the cattle stampeded." Its two independent clauses are joined by the conjunction "and."

concluding sentence. A sentence that provides an overall impression or synthesis of the information in a paragraph. May paraphrase the topic sentence.

cue. To give additional information to help a student produce a desired response.

direct instruction. Teaching that is instructor-directed and explicit regarding rules for language structure and expectations for student performance. Sometimes contrasted with child-centered, or child-led, instruction, which requires students to guess the rules for language structure.

essay. A short, usually analytic prose composition on a particular theme or subject, often comprised of more than one paragraph.

executive functions. The mental abilities to plan, organize, monitor, and self-regulate.

expository language. Language that explains and clarifies. Expository text makes information explicit. Language in subject-area textbooks is usually expository.

extrinsic. Coming from outside the individual. For example, a teacher may use extrinsic cueing strategies to prompt a student's response.

framework. A template or graphic organizer that outlines a sentence, paragraph, or essay structure; supports language production; and contains embedded cues that aid word retrieval and sentence formulation.

Landmark School, Inc.

intrinsic. Coming from within the individual. For example, students learn intrinsic cueing strategies for self-cueing.

kernel sentence. A minimal sentence comprised of a noun plus a verb. For example, "Sacajawea climbed."

language expression. The spoken or written production of language, including retrieval and formulation.

micro-unit. To break a complex task down into smaller, more easily mastered subtasks.

mnemonic. Pertaining to memory. Mnemonic devices are tools to enhance memory. For example, the mnemonic *m-a-d* aids recall of three adjective types (*m*ade of, *a*ge, *d*esign).

multisensory instruction. Teaching that provides inputs to multiple senses. Classic multisensory reading instruction teaches language patterns through visual, auditory, and kinesthetic modalities.

oral rehearsal. Oral practice formulating language prior to and during writing tasks.

paragraph. A group of sentences that expresses and supports a main idea.

phonological. Pertaining to speech sounds.

phonological processing. Pertaining to mental processing for speech formation.

script. The written text of an interaction between teacher and students.

self-correction. An individual's recognition and resolution of his or her own error. Valuable evidence of self-monitoring.

self-monitoring. Awareness and checking of one's own behavior to achieve desired outcomes. An aspect of executive functioning.

semantic. Pertaining to linguistic meaning. Finding a synonym is a semantic task, as it involves searching for an alternate word with the same meaning.

speech-language. The union of speech and language. Speech refers to oral communication, which involves processing and articulating speech sounds. Language refers to a communication system of spoken, written, or gestural symbols.

strand. Subtopic of a theme. For example, "southwest Indians" is a strand of the theme "Native Americans."

syntax. The rules that govern the order of words in sentences.

template. A skeletal structure that supports language production. Usually a visual outline.

theme. A topic of discourse or composition. A unifying or dominant idea. Can be broken down into strands and substrands.

topic sentence. The sentence that introduces the topic of a paragraph. In this book, the paragraph's first sentence.

verbal working memory. The mind's ability to hold verbal information temporarily in consciousness and to modify that information.

Bibliography

Appleby, A., and J. Langer. "Instructional Scaffolding: Reading and Writing as Natural Language Activities." In *Composing and Comprehending*, edited by J. Jensen. Urbana, IL: National Council of Teachers of English, 1984.

Bereiter, C. "Development in Writing." In *Cognitive Processes in Writing*, edited by L. Gregg and E. Steinberg. Hillsdale, NJ: Erlbaum, 1980.

Catts, H. "The Relationship between Speech-Language Impairments and Reading Disabilities." *Journal of Speech and Hearing Research* 36 (1993):948–58.

Catts, H., and A. Kamhi. "The Linguistic Basis of Reading Disorders: Implications for the Speech-Language Pathologist." *Language, Speech and Hearing in the Schools* 17 (1986):329–41.

Chall, J. *Stages of Reading Development*. New York: McGraw-Hill, 1983.

Chomsky, C. "Approaching Reading through Invented Spelling." In Vol. 2 of *Theory and Practice of Early Reading*, edited by L. Resnick and C. Weaver. Hillsdale, NJ: Erlbaum, 1979.

Clark, D., and L. Uhry. *Dyslexia: Theory and Practice of Remedial Instruction*. Baltimore: York, 1995.

Flood, J. *Handbook of Research on Teaching the English Language Arts*. New York: MacMillan, 1991.

Freeman, E., and D. Person, eds. *Using Nonfiction Trade Books in the Elementary Classroom from Ants to Zeppelins*. Urbana, IL: National Council of Teachers of English, 1992.

Hillocks, G. *Research in Written Composition: New Directions for Teaching*. Urbana, IL: ERIC Clearinghouse on Reading and Communication Skills, 1986.

Kamhi, A., and H. Catts. *Reading Disabilities: A Developmental Language Perspective*. Boston: Allyn & Bacon, 1991.

Langer, J., and A. Appleby. *How Writing Shapes Thinking*. Urbana, IL: National Council of Teachers of English, 1987.

Liberman, I., and A. Liberman. "Whole Language Versus Code Emphasis: Underlying Assumptions and Their Implications for Reading Instruction." *Annals of Dyslexia* 40 (1990):51–76.

Lyon, G.R., and N. Krasnegor. *Attention, Memory and Executive Function*. Baltimore: Brooks, 1996.

Lyon, R. "Learning Disabilities." *The Future of Children: Special Education for Students with Disabilities* 1 (1996):54–76.

Pehsson, R., and P. Denner. *Semantic Organizers: A Study Strategy for Special Needs Learners*. Rockville, MD: Aspen, 1989.

Pinker, S. *The Language Instinct: How the Mind Creates Language*. New York: Morrow, 1994.

Strong, W. *Creative Approaches to Sentence Combining*. Urbana, IL: National Council of Teachers of English, 1986.

Wallach, G., and K. Butler. *Language Learning Disabilities in School-Age Children and Adolescents*. New York: MacMillan, 1994.

SLIP SHEET!

SLIP SHEET!

SLIP SHEET!

SLIP SHEET!

SLIP SHEET!

SLIP SHEET!

SLIP SHEET!

SLIP SHEET!

SLIP SHEET!

SLIP SHEET!

SLIP SHEET!

SLIP SHEET!

SLIP SHEET!
SLIP SHEET!
SLIP SHEET!
SLIP SHEET!
SLIP SHEET!
SLIP SHEET!
SLIP SHEET!

SLIP SHEET! SLIP SHEET! SLIP SHEET!

SLIP SHEET! SLIP SHEET!